Tapestry of Love
Poetry of Faith, Hope and Love

Janice Crosby Short

PublishAmerica
Baltimore

© 2007 by Janice Crosby Short.
All rights reserved. No part of this book may be reproduced, stored in a retrieval system or transmitted in any form or by any means without the prior written permission of the publishers, except by a reviewer who may quote brief passages in a review to be printed in a newspaper, magazine or journal.

First printing

ISBN: 1-4241-7176-8
PUBLISHED BY PUBLISHAMERICA, LLLP
www.publishamerica.com
Baltimore

Printed in the United States of America

To my husband and editor, Clyde
My four children and grandchildren
Who fill my life with wonder, love, and challenges

MY HEART IS OVERFLOWING WITH A BEAUTIFUL
THOUGHT! I WILL WRITE A LOVELY POEM TO THE KING,
FOR I AM AS FULL OF WORDS AS THE SPEEDIEST
WRITER POURING OUT HIS STORY.
PSALMS 45:1

A GRAIN OF SAND IN THE HOURGLASS

Inside each of us is a kingdom…
Uniquely woven by faith in God's Son.
Holds no care, anxiety, or fear…
In this world that is slowly moving on.

As a grain of sand in the hourglass…
Quietly slipping away.
The earthly vessel that formed this flesh…
Was never meant to stay.

Inside each of us is an eternity of…
God's gift of Love, Truth, and Grace.
Holding on to this world is…
Simply foolish and a disgrace.

The living will—the testament of eternal life…
The gift in God's Beloved Son.
Overcame earth's groans of struggle, and strife.
When the work of God's Son was done.

Eternal life is in God's Truth and Grace…
After Father Time takes back
The sands of time in the hourglass.
There will be no want or lack.

> Peace be still; O my soul!
> You are a grain of sand in the hourglass.
> Your eternal abiding place…
> Is in God's Love, Truth, and Grace.

RAINBOW:
And the Lord God formed man of the dust of the ground, and breathed into his nostrils the breath of life; and man became a living soul.
Gen 2:7

And this is the record, that God hath given to us eternal life, and this life is in His Son.
1 John 5:11

SURRENDER

Dear God,

Take my darkness of doubts away.
I am tired, lonely, and have lost my way.
My soul is sick, weary, and heavy-laden.
My eyes grow dim as the day is fading.

Teach me about God and the Savior…
That I might find Your Love and favor.
Give me a life that I might know.
That You are with me—wherever I go.

Mold me according to Your perfect will.
Speak to my heart—peace be still.
Give me faith to meet my needs.
While I am seeking truth on bended knees.

Let me sit at Jesus' feet—look on His face.
Trust in His Word of Truth and Grace.
My eyes to behold His redemptive plan.
While I am holding on to His nail-scarred hand.

Deliver me from all doubts and fears.
Wipe away all my sadness and tears.
Be my true Lover and faithful Friend.
Guide me through this world of temptation and sin.

Heal my broken heart from hurt and pain.
My confidence and loyalty in you I will gain.
Keep my eyes focused upon Your Heavenly plan.
The redemption of earth for fallen man.

Search me, O Lord—let there be no other.
Be my Teacher, Comfort, Guide, and Lover.
Give birth to my heart in the words of Your son.
Your Kingdom come—Your will be done.

RAINBOW:
For great is Your love, higher than the heavens; your faithfulness reaches to the skies. Be exalted, O God, above the heavens, and let Your glory be over all the earth. Save us and help us with Your right hand, that those You love may be delivered.
Psalms 108:4-8

ANGELS – RAINBOWS – BUTTERFLYS

When you are cast down, O my soul…
Look to the universe as one whole.
Look inward, look outward, look upward and look down.
Look for butterflies, rainbows, and angels with crowns.

Look for the cattle on a thousand hills.
Look for turtles, frogs, kittens, and whip-poor-wills.
For majestic mountains, rivers, and streams.
And rainbows, butterflies, and angels with wings.

Look to the winter when the cold winds blow.
Look for rain, sleet, ice, and snow.
Look to the fall when the leaves are on the ground.
Look for rainbows, butterflies, and angels all around.

Look at the trees when the leaves are green.
Look for resurrection of life in the spring.
Look for roots of love and faith with wings.
And butterflies, and rainbows, and angels and things.

Look to the east and look to the west.
Look for God, who loves us the best.
Look at the moon, the galaxies of stars in the sky.
Look for a rainbow, an angel and a butterfly.

When you are all alone and your soul is cast down.
Your body is weary and your face wears a frown.
Look inward and upward through the skies.
For rainbows, angels, and butterflies.

RAINBOW:
And instantly I was, in spirit, there in heaven and saw—oh, the glory of it!—a throne and someone sitting on it! Great bursts of light flashed forth from Him as from a glittering diamond, or from a shining ruby, and a rainbow glowing like an emerald encircled His throne.
Revelation 4:2-3

In Memory of Debra Holmes, who left us rainbows.

BEAUTIFUL FEET

Beautiful are the feet of Jesus.
Beautiful is the Lamb of God.
Beautiful are the feet of Jesus.
Earth blessed where His feet have trod.

He sowed the seed of righteousness.
He sowed the seed of love.
He sowed the seed of Truth and Grace.
His heart was from above.

His feet tread out humility.
The salt and light of the world.
The seed of life and liberty.
Where peace and love is heard.

Mary took a pound of ointment.
Wiped them with her hair.
Kissed the feet of Jesus.
Fragrance filled the air.

Jesus said to His disciples.
I wash your feet to tread.
The righteous seed of life.
Living water and pure bread.

Beautiful are the feet of those…
Who make "The Word" supreme.
Who bring good tidings to the earth.
That God still rules and reigns.

RAINBOW:
How beautiful upon the mountains are the feet of him that brings good news. Who proclaim peace, who bring good tidings, who proclaim salvation, who say to Zion. "Your God reigns!"
Isaiah 52:7

Dedicated to my daughter Joni, who is battling multiple sclerosis; and is more than a conqueror through Jesus Christ our Lord.

BEGIN AGAIN

There is a place in your heart that only God can fill.
Begin to open your heart for God's will.
God knows your struggles to survive on earth…
This is the reason for your spiritual birth.

Sometimes His voice is quiet, sometimes loud.
Sometimes it is covered with a sin-dark cloud.
One day you will see if you never give up…
From reading the pages of His Holy Book.

One day at a time—read His word…
Then the music will happen with the sounds of the birds.
Be careful to listen and open your heart…
For Jesus is standing outside in the dark.

He opens the way to Heaven and the discovery is gold…
For the hungry heart and the sin-sick soul.
All the beauty of Holiness we cannot explain…
God has put it all in Jesus' name.

All of our senses are to be focused on Him…
The Savior, Redeemer, and Forever Friend.
Grow a little closer each day as you walk…
Give yourself time to visit and talk.

The seed in the heart will continue to grow…
As you feed on the Word, the Word will flow.
Like rivers of water that never cease…
The Love for God will expand and increase.

When Jesus consumes all of the heart…
The light will expose the sin in the dark.
No fear of evil will ever be known…
Where His righteous seed has been sown.

The birth of the baby born in Bethlehem…
Will continue to grow until you are like Him…
Begin again—Begin again…
There is no failure in Jesus, our friend.

RAINBOW:
No, in all these things we are more than conquerors through Him who loved us.
Romans 8:37

Dedicated to all the strugglers who are living on earth.

BEHOLD THE LAMB

Behold! The spotless Lamb of God…
Whose feet upon this earth have trod.
The righteous seed for sinful man…
To stand before "The Great I Am."

Through eternity, time, and space…
God enclosed the human race.
Through fire, water, land, and sea…
Heaven joins earth to eternity.

Through His blood – the flesh does cry…
Lord, unclean—unclean—am I.
Purify me in Your Holy Love…
With the Lamb's spotless blood.

Open my eyes that I might see…
The Lamb of God at Calvary.
His nail-scarred hands—his sword-pierced side…
His crimson blood flowing deep and wide.

Behold! The spotless Lamb…
Who was and is…"The Great I Am."
Who gave His life—so we could be…
With God's Love through eternity.

RAINBOW:
For you know that it was not with perishable things such as silver or gold that you were redeemed from the empty way of life handed down to you from our forefathers, but with the precious blood of Christ, a lamb without blemish or defect.
1 Peter 1:18-19

BREAD OF LIFE

Jesus said, "I have food to eat that you know nothing of…
I speak of spiritual food from the Heavens above.
The words that I speak are truth and life…
Coming from My Father's throne room on high."

Words still come from our loving Savior.
Words that are filled with God's Love and favor.
Words, wonderful words of Truth and Grace.
Beautiful words God sends to the human race.

Words that bless and bring peace and joy.
Words that the world cannot destroy.
God gave the kingdom of this world to Him…
To bring us to the truth of an age without end.

He gave us an invitation to come eat and dine…
Where there's plenty of food all the time.
Eating Jesus' words of His flesh and blood…
We are a branch in the vine of God's Infinite Love.

Jesus owns all the kingdoms in this world below.
He was clothed in humanity—so God could bestow…
To the inward man—the bread of Heaven.
Pure words of life—love without leaven.

Words of the Master, pure, sincere, faithful, and true…
Sending His blessing for me and you.
Sharing His Kingdom of Grace, Power, and Glory.
Written in blood through the pages of God's story.

Eating Jesus' flesh and drinking His blood…
Brings us Heaven's bread of God's pure Love.
There is living water coming from the throne.
Heavenly places this world has never known.

The mind of Christ is the heart of God.
He shares with the earth God's Kingdom of Love.
His thoughts and ways are not our own.
God feeds our spirit through the blood of His Son.

We are His children—the sheep of His fold…
Reaping the Redeemer's bread in the pages of old.
His Kingdom is built on God's power and glory.
We, His children, sigh, Holy, Holy, Holy.

RAINBOW:
But in the meantime His disciples besought Him, saying, Master, eat, But He said unto them, I have food to eat that ye know not of.
John 4:31-32

CHANGE

Seconds change to minutes.
Minutes change to hours.
Hours change to weeks.
Weeks change to months.
Months change to years.
Then it starts all over.

Winter changes to spring.
Spring changes to summer.
Summer changes to fall.
Then it starts all over.

Morning changes to noon.
Noon changes to evening.
Evening changes to night.
Night changes to morning.
Then it starts all over.

Baby changes to child.
Child changes to youth.
Youth changes to adult.
Adult changes to old age.
Old age changes in death.
Then it starts all over.

God changes not.
He is always the same.
The Creator—The Word.
The Potter—The Vinedresser.
The Alpha—The Omega.
The Savior—The Redeemer.
The Bridegroom—The Kingdom.
The Power—The Glory.
Eternity.
Salvation's Story

RAINBOW:
Listen, I tell you a mystery: We will not all sleep, but we will all be changed—in a flash, in the twinkling of an eye, at the last trumpet. For the trumpet will sound, the dead will be raised imperishable and we will be changed.
1 Corinthians 15:51-52

I thee Lord do not change. So you, O descendants of Jacob, are not destroyed.
Malachi 3:6

CHRISTIAN'S PEACE

There is only one, Jesus explained…
There is only one in God's Holy Name.
One Spirit, One heart, One Mind…
Love rules the universe in space and in time.

One who thinks and speaks Truth and Grace…
One that covered the sins of the human race.
We are all blood brothers in this world below…
Only Jesus' blood washes us whiter than snow.

We are all one in God's Great Universe…
We think and create a blessing or a curse.
The mind of Jesus, so pure and so true…
Was God's gift to humanity to make all things new.

He is the Potter and we are the clay…
He molds us and makes us day by day.
Joining our Spirit to His perfect Love…
Feeding us truth from the Heavens above.

God's thoughts and ways are not our own…
They come from one seed the Master has sown.
God's righteous seed that is planted within…
Gives us faith in our Savior who took away sin.

Faith moves mountains of doubts and fears…
Love conquers all and wipes away tears.
Life is eternal, O death, where is your sting?
There is only one body where the church bells ring.

Jesus' blood covers a multitude of our sins…
The Lover of our soul and our very best Friend.
When you think you are alone and feel very sad…
Faith in God's Love will make you very glad.

So search the Scriptures to find this great light…
That gives fallen humanity the gift of pure sight.
What more can we say—what more can we do…
But give our allegiance to the Faithful and True.

Seeking God's Love more precious than gold…
Finding one heart, one mind, one soul.
He created us one in this great universe…
By taking our sin, our guilt, and our curse.

RAINBOW:
We are no longer Jews, or Greeks or slaves or free men or even merely men or women, but we are all the same. We are Christians: we are one in Christ Jesus.
Ephesians 3:28

COME – TASTE – AND SEE

We all came to earth full of lust and pride…
With a place in our soul where sin can hide.
We all stand guilty of sin, shame, and disgrace…
Until we find Jesus, who took sin's place.

It is His blood that cleanses the soul.
It is His Love that has fire of pure gold.
Wisdom, strength, power, honor, and glory…
Is hidden in Christ—the one true life story.

We all need Jesus—the faithful and true.
To cleanse our soul with His blood that is pure.
God calls us to eat from His wisdom and grace.
The King's table is set—come, see, and taste.

By eating His flesh and drinking His blood …
We have communion with our Father of Love.
The flesh is bread and His blood is pure wine.
The table is set where there is love all the time.

The earth and Heaven is joined by the cross.
The Shepherd is calling for sheep that are lost.
He is seeking the ones, strayed from His fold…
To bind their wounds with love of pure gold.

Come, taste, and see—our Savior's call.
There is food for one—there is food for all.
This food is not polluted and tainted with sin…
It is filled with God's Spirit—where Love has no end.

RAINBOW:

Taste and see that the Lord is good; blessed is the man who takes refuge in Him.
Psalms 34:8

COMMON AND HOLY GROUND

We are one standing on common ground.
Searching and seeking and looking around.
Eating old bread and rejecting the new.
The Faithful—The Just—The sacred—The True.

We are born naked, poor, wretched, and blind…
Without Christ's righteousness and God's Love Divine.
Without God's peace, power, and pure love.
So God created a plan from the Heavens above.

To live and breathe and have our being in Him…
The Holy One, who came to earth without sin.
Jesus, the Savior, the name of renown.
Shows us "The Way" to live on Holy Ground.

He keeps our souls hungering and thirsting for the True…
Until all things in us have been made new.
Our soul in its darkness is drawn to God's Light…
Turning our blindness into pure sight.

Our prayers of groaning and sighing and call…
Seeks the Redeemer who frees us from "The Fall"…
Of doubts, worries, anxieties, and fears…
We cry, "Abba Father," be very near.

In confidence—in quietness—in silence—and still…
We seek "The Divine," we seek God's will.
In sorrow and suffering—in tears, we cry…
We seek redemption with our inner eye.

God made us in His image and likeness, you see…
He loves us so much—He wants us set free.
With Christ's body, His blood, and His soul…
God's gift of "Heaven's Bread" to make us whole.

The bread is Holy—The blood is new wine…
The bread and drink is God's covenant sublime.
God works for our good in His Divine plan…
He is the Master Builder with the nail-scarred hands.

His word is an anvil—an axe, you see…
God is pruning away the old, corrupt tree.
To give us a new and better way from His roots of love…
A new heart and mind from the Heavens above.

RAINBOW:
And all that believed were together, and had all things common.
Acts 2:44

Having therefore, brethren, boldness to enter into the holiest by the blood of Jesus.
Hebrew 10:19

CONFRONTATION

Who put wisdom in the inward parts?
Who gives understanding to the hearts?

Who provides for the raven and its prey?
Who changes the night to day?

Where is the place where the lights dwell?
How does the water from the oceans swell?

What are the ordinances of Heaven above?
Can you set its dominion in the earth with love?

God answered Job in his despair...
When I laid earth's foundation—were you there?

How—who—what—where—when...
They all came forth as a mighty wind.

From the dry and desert sand...
Answer Me, Job, if you can.

We, like Job, have questions, too...
Some are reality and some are true.

God has given us the answer in "The God Man"…
Who came from "The Father" so we could understand.

How much He loves and wants us to know Him…
By giving us "The Living Word" to cleanse us from sin.

RAINBOW:
The Lord said to Job: "Will the one who contends with the Almighty correct Him?
Let him who accused God answer Him!"
Job 40:1

CONVERSATION WITH GOD

Where are You, God?
Why am I here?
This world is too big…
I am lost…
How can I know?
Where do I go?
When will I know?
Answer me, Lord, as You did…
Moses, in the burning bush.
Jonah, in the belly of the whale.
Gideon, threshing wheat in the wine press.
Job, as he sat among the ashes.
Paul, on the road to Damascus.
Mary, searching for You after Your burial.
Hannah, when You promised her a child.
The disciples on the stormy sea.
The woman at the well.
Abraham, the father of faith.
Sarah, as she waited for the promise of Isaac.
John, on the island of Patmos.
I am a child of darkness, pain, and suffering.
I need security, direction, and protection.
I face many enemies…
Wars, fighting, jealousy, hate…
Fears, anxieties, divisions, and broken hearts…
Darkness, deceptions, sickness, death, and destruction.

I am like a wandering sheep without a shepherd.
I am in bondage to the flesh…
Weakness, poverty, darkness, deception…
Ignorance, money, lust, and pride.
Where are You, God?
Speak to me…
I need Your…
Strength
Love
Joy
Truth
Grace
Understanding.
Peace
Faith
Hope

RAINBOW:
Where can I go from Your spirit? Where can I flee from Your presence? If I go up to the heavens, You are there; if I make my bed in the depths, you are there.
Psalms 139:7-8

CRUCIFIED WITH CHRIST

When I surveyed the old, rugged cross...
And the hill to Mount Calvary...
The Saints who counted all things loss...
And their songs of victory.

I ask God to crucify me...
As He did in the flesh of His Son.
To give me His life on earth...
So my Lord and I could be one.

I felt no pain of the nails in my hands...
Nor the sword that pierced His side.
The blood that flowed down Calvary's hill...
To my heart He joyfully applied.

With God's Love and peace all around...
My blinded eyes could now see.
This house of flesh—from Adam's first sin...
Gave way to eternity.

Clothed in God's righteousness...
By the Incarnate Word of "The Son"...
My heart is set on Heaven...
When my work on earth is done.

RAINBOW:
Knowing this, that the old man is crucified with Him, that the body of sin might be destroyed, that henceforth we should not serve sin.
Romans 6:6

CRY OF THE FLESH

Where can I go from this world of deception and sin…
To feed my poor spirit—my broken heart mend?
Where can I go in my fears' darkest hour…
To receive love, comfort, truth, and power.

Where can I go when I am in despair…
To find comfort, hope, and someone to care?
Where can I go when I am alone…
From the comfort of family, friends, and home?

Where can I find peace in earth's turmoil…
Rest from my burdens, labor, and toil?
When life is fearful and war is inevitable..
Where can I hide—a place that's infallible?

In my hurt, pain, grief, and sorrow…
Where is the promise of a better tomorrow?
This flesh I've inherited from the human race…
Where can I go to find life's resting place?

The answer will come—oh yes, you will see…
Behold! God's infallible Word is Heaven's trinity.
Reach beyond the Heaven to "The Spirit's Eye."
God sees—God knows—God hears the flesh's cry.

The cry of our flesh—Jesus understands.
God has put all in His Holy hands.
While we live this earthly flesh—the Spirit hears our cry…
Trust God's infallible Word—there's power from on high.

RAINBOW:
The Lord is my rock, and my fortress, and my deliverer; my God is my rock, in whom I take refuge. He is my shield, and the horn of my salvation, and my stronghold.
Psalms 18:2

DAY DAWNING

There is a day not known by man.
The day that is in God's almighty hand.
No one knows the day nor the hour.
When Jesus returns with glory and power.

To rule and reign in truth and righteousness.
The earth will be filled with His blessedness.
All eyes will be focused on Him…
The soul's Lover, Redeemer, and Friend.

The day is dawning—the star is rising in our hearts.
When the good prevails and the evil departs.
The sunrise and dawning of that great day.
Souls rejoicing in the Son's glorious ray.

The light that now shines in the dark place.
Will rule and reign over the human race.
Search me, O Lord, and know my heart.
See if there is any evil hiding in the dark.

Let my focus be upon the day of "The Son."
When the day spring opens to "The Holy One."
Who gave His life to set us free.
From sin's death—and life's captivity.

The day is dawning and drawing very near.
When grief, sorrow, and pain will no longer appear.
We will forever rejoice in the return of the Son.
The day spring will arise and earth's battles will be won.

RAINBOW:
Early in the morning, before the sun is up. I am praying and pointing out how much I trust in you. I stay awake through the night to think about your promises. Because you are so loving and kind, listen to me and make me well again.
Psalms 119:147-149

DAY STAR

When I have fears that I will cease to be…
I look to the Day Star of Infinity.

Trillions of stars are numbered and named in the sky…
Never to be seen by man's mortal eye.

God spoke to one man named Abraham…
Who fathered the faith to "The Great I Am"

At a very old age you will father a son…
A seed from your loin will come forth, "The Holy One."

Numbered by the sand and the stars in the sky…
The soul will be guided by "The Star" from on high.

One bright "Day Star" led the wise men…
To a baby's cradle in Bethlehem.

One "Day Star" from the Heavens above…
Came to earth cradled by God's Infinite Love.

Each individual has a soul of their own…
The "Day Star" to guide them to their heavenly home.

God's invitation to come through "The Door" of the fold…
To be shepherded as sheep by "The Star" in their soul.

Abraham's seed brings God's children from afar.
To be numbered and named by "The Celestial Star."

When I am afraid I will look back to Calvary...
And remember "The Star" who died for me.

"One Star" resurrected from the dead...
So God's earthly children could be heavenly fed.

RAINBOW:
We have also a more sure word of prophecy, unto which you do well that you take heed as unto a light that shines in a dark place, until the day dawn, and the day star arise in your hearts.
2 Peter. 1:19

DIVINE LOVE

God loves me—God loves you…
With a love that is pure, faithful, and true.
Pouring His love into all creation…
Built on Truth and Grace—The Spirit's foundation.

Lasting, enduring, never offended…
God's Love can never be comprehended.
Without wax, false covering, and fear.
He comforts our grief and wipes away each tear.

God's Love comes from the passion of His Son.
O grave, where is your victory—life's battle is won.
God gave His life for this great treasure.
Enduring Grace and Truth with eternal measure.

Pure Holy Love—tested and tried by fire.
Arrows piercing hearts with flames to inspire.
Sealed by His Spirit—God's name glorified.
Cleansing souls—Love magnified.

A legacy of faith—life's undying history.
Uniting humanity to this great mystery.
Built on the Son's obedience, faith, truth, and trust.
Love never fades, decays, or rusts.

Written in blood by God's beloved Son.
The battle for life was victoriously won.
Blotting out our transgressions and sin.
Alpha, Omega, with no beginning or end.

RAINBOW:
My purpose is that they may be encouraged in heart and united in love, so that they may have the full riches of complete understanding, in order that they may know the mystery of God, namely, Christ, in whom are hidden all the treasures of wisdom and knowledge.
Colossians 2: 2-3

EARTH'S GREATEST BATTLE

Jesus came to earth in glory and power...
Earth's Savior, Redeemer, and Friend.
Victory for humanity in His final hour...
When sin's darkness was placed on Him.

We find the enemy of the earth...
Waiting to take hold of Him.
In a manger "God the Son" lay at birth...
Holy, pure, unjustly condemned.

Sin's death was lurking to employ...
Earth's enemy was close at hand.
Waiting to kill, steal, and destroy...
The Son of God—the son of man.

Earth's tempter, the father of lies...
Sought to destroy Heaven's Truth and Grace.
With pride, lust of flesh, and eyes...
Was the great deceiver of the human race.

The Holy Child of Truth and Grace...
Never yielded to the temptation of sin.
Winning the great battle for the human race...
Never letting the light of the Father grow dim.

Sorrows of earth—joy of Heaven…
Gave birth to God's Holy seed.
In His birth, life, death, and resurrection…
He feels our infirmities and knows our ever need.

His Grace and Truth is our salvation…
We glean from the pages of His love story.
The master and creator of all creation…
In fear and wonder we sigh—Holy, Holy, Holy.

Never more to wander…
In the deception and darkness of sin.
Finding the light of a loving Savior…
To put our trust and confidence in.

Jesus has clothed us in His righteousness.
His blood has set us free from the curse.
Earth's greatest battle was won…
The great deceiver has no hold on us.

RAINBOW:
In whom we have redemption through His blood, the forgiveness of sins, according to the riches of His grace.
Ephesians 1:7

EASTER

God has given us a day of hope…
In the resurrection of His Son.
The gift of His life's story…
When His work on earth was done.

His resurrection became a symbol…
To the earth below.
As the pages to His story…
Reveals the righteous seed He sowed.

Faith—Hope—Love.
We glean from His Incarnate Word.
The seed of eternal life.
The sweetest music one's soul has ever heard.

He has given to us "The Promise"…
Sent from the Father above.
A message through redemption…
Of God's eternal Love.

His blood fell upon the earth.
His seed sown in the ground.
Shouts of victory, "He is Risen"…
When His earthly body was found.

He returned and walked on earth...
To complete the Father's love story.
They watched Him return to Heaven...
In clouds of great glory.

They heard the angels...
Speaking in a loud voice.
This same Jesus will return.
Rejoice! Rejoice! Rejoice!

RAINBOW:
As they were straining their eyes for another glimpse, suddenly two white-robed men were standing there among them, and said, "Men of Galilee, why are you standing here staring at the sky? Jesus has gone away to heaven, and some day, just as He went, he will return!
Acts 1:10-11

EMOTIONS

My mind is troubled…
My hearts in despair.
My soul is searching.
Lord, are You there?

Pain attacks my body…
Darkness is near.
Fear is present.
Doubts fill the air.

My heart seeks "The Word"…
Have faith in God's Son…
Life's battle is over.
Victoriously won.

Be strong and of good courage…
Find your rest in God's Infallible Word.
I have given you His Spirit.
God's truth—you have heard.

There is always a song to sing…
Always a church bell to ring.
Joy unspeakable—full of God's glory.
Giving birth to the Savior's life story.

Be still and know—that I am God…
Grace and Truth—your Redeemer has trod.
The gift of the Righteous Seed.
That will meet your every need.

RAINBOW:
So we fix our eyes not on what we have seen, but on what is unseen. For what is seen is temporary, but what is unseen is eternal.
2 Corinthians 4:18

EXALTATION OF JESUS

Wonderful and magnificent are the works of God's hand.
The Creator of heaven, earth, sea, and land.
Greater still is the Living Word of His voice.
By faith, our fearful hearts are made to rejoice.

In our trials of suffering, grief, pain, and sorrow…
God's Word gives us hope for a better tomorrow.
In Heaven's view of faith, love, joy, peace, and hope…
We see through the eye of a broader telescope.

Flesh and Spirit coming together as one…
In the redemption of earth, through God's begotten Son.
Lust and pride was crucified by Truth and Grace…
With a higher exaltation for the human soul.

We are one soul in God's universe.
Heaven blessing the earth from nature's curse.
Coming together through the cross of His Son.
God exalting His Love through "The Holy One."

Glory, honor, worship, exaltation, and praise…
To Heaven's Son whom God raised.
From death to life through the cross and His Word.
One Spirit—One Lord—One God—One Father—we serve.

RAINBOW:
There God exalted Him to the highest place and gave Him the name that is above every name, that at the name of Jesus every knee should bow, in heaven and on earth and under the earth, and every tongue confess that Jesus Christ is Lord to the glory of God the Father.
Philippians 29-11

FAITH IN GOD

Above all of earth's possession…
Above all knowledge and understanding…
God has given us a gift
That cannot be comprehended.

The gift of His Holy Spirit…
That would join us to our Creator.
In Grace, Truth, and Righteousness.
Life's scapegoat, intercessor, and mediator.

God's Love overcame the world
And helps us not to go astray.
Keeps us away from temptations…
And the evil of the day.

He has to be Lord…
In all that we do.
Faith working through me.
Faith working through you.

RAINBOW:
Everyone born of God overcomes the world. This is the victory that has overcome the world. even our faith.
1 John 5:4

FAMILY PRAYER

May the beauty of Jesus' righteousness…
Fill our home with joy and peace.
May our thoughts and ways be pure…
God's Holy Spirit increase.

May the mind of Christ be in us…
His truth guide our ways.
May all the darkness be dispersed…
And our voices be filled with praise.

May we count our every blessing…
That comes from Jesus' light.
May the radiance of His countenance…
Give our hearts spiritual sight.

May we be filled with His presence…
Established in His Immaculate Love.
May every thought be taken captive…
To our Father's will above.

May the glory of His Son…
Fill the earth, land, and sea.
May His Kingdom come to reign…
In our hearts through eternity.

May we acknowledge Him…
In all our thoughts, words, and deeds.
From the seed of His righteousness…
May His Spirit lead.

May no thoughts of evil…
Come near the door of our mind.
Keep us away from earth's temptation…
With Truth and Love Divine.

May our body be…
The dwelling place of God.
In Grace and Truth's protection…
By His staff and by His rod.

RAINBOW:
For this reason I kneel before the Father, from whom the whole family in heaven and on earth derives its name.
Ephesians 3:14

FINDING IT ALL

Finding it all in Jesus…
Earth's Lord, Savior, Redeemer and King.
Finding "The Gift of God"…
In the message that Jesus brings.

I found the hidden manna of Heaven…
In the sounds of silence I heard.
The sights and sounds of all creation…
When I tasted "The Living Word."

I drank from His fountain of living water…
And it quenched the thirst of my soul.
In the spirit of my Savior…
My life is complete and made whole.

My soul longs for God's presence.
In the night and in the day.
Keep me close to You, O Holy Spirit…
Never let me go astray.

I found Grace, Truth, and Love…
In the life of God's righteous Son.
I pray daily, not my will, Father,
But Your will be done.

In the cross of Calvary...
I found the joy in suffering on earth.
In the resurrection of Jesus' death.
I found His presence in the new birth.

Master of all things great and small...
Teach me how to love without sin.
In my thoughts, words, and deeds...
Never let me criticize, judge, or condemn.

I found it all in Jesus...
God's Kingdom, power, and glory.
I tasted and gleaned the hidden manna...
From the pages of His infinite story.

RAINBOW:
There is one Body, and one Spirit, just as you were called—One Lord, one Faith, one Baptism; one God and Father of all, who is over all and through all and in all.
Ephesians 4:4-6

FOOD FOR THOUGHT

Feeding our thoughts from the Savior's mind.
Finding a sweet-smelling savor all the time.
Trusting in His Holy Word, faithful and pure.
We eat Heaven's manna year after year.

Finding God's heart in the center of the universe.
Brings sweet blessings from nature's curse.
Redeeming the earth through one great mind
Reveals the Kingdom of eternity, space, and time.

With God's gift of Truth and Grace.
The cross transformed the human race.
Bringing us together under God's Love.
Through one Holy seed from Heavens above.

As the rain comes down and the snow from Heaven.
Watering the seed both leaven and unleavened.
That it may bring forth and bud…
God's righteous seed from the Savior's Love.

The true and faithful Friend supplies our needs.
Riches, glory, and honor from His Holy seed.
Peace and righteousness kissed—Heaven and earth sings.
To the Lord of lords and the King of kings.

Worship and praise with thanksgiving and song…
Our hearts are made to be glad all the day long.
God has given us "One Name" above every name.
His Love transforms and always the same.

RAINBOW:
And the angel said unto her, "Do not be afraid, Mary, you have found favor with God. You will be with child and give birth to a son, and you are to give Him the name Jesus. He will be great and will be called the Son of the Most High. The Lord God will give Him the throne of His father, David, and He will reign over the house of Jacob forever, his kingdom will never end."
Luke 30:33

FOREVER LOVED

In the sunshine and in the rain.
In the winter and in the spring.
In the earth, heaven, sea, and sky…
God's Love will never die.
On the mountains high and in the valley's slope.
In death and destruction; God gives us hope.
In the morning light and the evening shade.
From the cradle to the grave.
Forever loved is the angel's song.
In the night and all day long.
Joy unspeakable and full of glory…
Is God's pure Love in Jesus' story.
He came as a baby in a garment of flesh.
To clothe us in His righteousness.
Not life—not death can take it away.
Jesus—our rock—our shield—our fortress—our stay.
He poured out His soul for the offering of sin.
In all of earth's battles His Love will win.
God's Love will endure—God's Love will prevail…
This is the story that Jesus does tell.
No one could love us with such splendor as this.
His Living Word brings joy, peace, power, and bliss.
His Love continues in our trials, grief, suffering, and sorrow.
Faith, hope, and love waits for a greater tomorrow.
This inheritance was given to you and to me.
God's Infinite Love sets our spirit free.

Free from life's burdens cares, anxieties, and fears.
From all of our sorrows, grief, sadness, and tears.
The beauty in His Holiness—we can never explain.
God's love for humanity is in Jesus' name.
He opened the door to God's throne on high…
On wings of faith—we learn how to fly.
His Grace is sufficient—His Love is pure gold.
He is preparing a place for our eternal soul.
Be still, O my soul—find peace and rest.
Jesus is our Sabbath—God gave us His best.

RAINBOW:
There is no fear in love. But perfect love drives out fear, because fear has to do with punishment. The one who fears is not made perfect in love. We love because He first loved us.
1 John 4:18-19

FROM CALVARY'S CROSS

From the cross Jesus bore…
To the crown of thorns He wore.
We are never alone…
Christ seats us with Him on Heaven's throne.

Though our sins be as scarlet…
They shall be white as snow.
Though they may be a multitude…
His word is written—that we might know.

From His death—we died.
From His resurrection—we live.
From His breath—we breathe.
From His peace—our heart is made still.

From His glory—we are crowned.
From His doctrine—we are sound.
From His heart—our hearts believes.
From His truth—His Grace is received.

Though we are lonely, poor, naked, and blind.
From His blood—we drank pure wine.
From His flesh—we eat Heaven's bread.
From His Spirit—we are tenderly led.

From His cross—our burdens He bears.
From His love—our sorrow He shares.
From His light—our way never grows dim.
Our heart keeps singing and rejoicing in Him.

From His Word—our faith does abound.
From His purity—we stand on Holy ground.
From His joy—our cup overflows.
From His valley—our soul He restores.

Our spirit does soar from His mountain.
Our thirst is quenched from His fountain.
From His story—Heaven and earth sing.
From His body—the church bells ring.

We will gladly cling to the old, rugged cross.
For Heaven is our gain and the earth is our loss.
We surrender the great battle to God and His infinite will.
And be glad of—His Cross—His Sword—His Shield.

RAINBOW:
And God raised us up with Christ and seated us with Him in the heavenly realms in Christ Jesus.
Ephesians 2:6

GIFTS

In the seed of Truth and Grace…
New life in Christ has begun.
Let us feed upon His Spirit…
Until each day is done.

Each day the bread of Heaven…
From God's heart of Love Divine.
Comes life from His Holy Spirit…
Through the gift of Father Time.

God faithfully replenishes Mother Earth…
In the seas, oceans, and lands.
From the celestial globe of the Heavens…
Come forth the works of His hands.

Mother Nature opens her arms…
To receive the gifts of truth and love.
She gives the gifts to her children…
As she sings to the Heavens above.

While we count our gifts one by one…
As many as the sands of time.
We celebrate God coming to earth…
Through our hearts and through our minds.

God gives us signs, miracles, and wonders…
In seeking His heart and mind.
Through His glory and through His suffering…
We share His gift of Father Time.

There is none righteous and no one is exempt…
From the pain and sufferings of earth.
In God's Love for humanity…
He gave us "The Gift" of His spiritual birth.

Everything is a gift from Heaven…
That God bestows on us with Love.
He purges it with His Truth and Grace…
From the Lamb's spotless blood.

RAINBOW:
Now if we are children, then we are heirs—heirs of God and co-heirs with Christ, if indeed we share in His sufferings in order that we may also share in His glory.
Romans 8:17

GOD'S WONDERFUL WAY

Though I am limited in this body of clay…
God has given me a marvelous, wonderful way…
Of helping me grow in thought, word, and deed…
Through millions of words I have learned to read.

I don't even have to be on the scene.
He has given me visions, hopes, and dreams.
He has helped me cross millions of miles.
Through hearts and minds of other lifestyles.

I have read many books since I was a child…
Mysteries, biographies, histories, legends, and profiles…
Allegories, symbols, fiction, non-fiction, and inspiration…
People, places, and things from generation to generation.

I have traveled many a mile since I learned to read…
Transforming, molding, my life's thoughts and deeds.
There is one Book that stands out above all…
God's Holy Word for the great and the small.

The Book has planted many a righteous seed…
Deep within my heart and supplies my every need.
I have walked in the garden at the cool of the day…
With God, Adam, and Eve in the Son's ray.

I have walked with Cain as a wanderer and vagabond…
Far away from the presence of God and His son.
I have traveled with Abraham—crossed many miles of land…
Looking for that city God built without hands.

I have wandered in the wilderness for many years…
Grumbling and complaining, shedding many tears.
I have sat with Gideon behind this wall of flesh…
Living in fear and trembling—entangled in mesh.

I have sat with Job in sackcloth and ashes…
Three friends who question his fate and his lashes.
I have walked with Isaac, David, and Ishmael…
Jacob, Rebecca, Hannah, Samuel.

With saints, and sinners I am well acquainted…
Seeing visions, hopes, and dreams the Master has painted.
I have sat and learned with Mary at the Lord's feet…
Saw Him pour out His soul on earth—so we could eat.

I have gleaned the field with Ruth—Boaz her redeemer…
Comforted by the words of Joseph—the dreamer…
And found fresh bread and new wine for the soul…
More knowledge and wealth than my mind can hold.

I have journeyed with the patriots and prophets of old…
Listened to their wisdom—words of pure gold…
Weaving together the covenant old and new…
Heaven blessing earth with a Son pure and true.

I have traveled with the disciples as they walked with the Lord…
Seeing signs, miracles, and wonders of God's Anointed One.
I have felt the heart of Peter—when his Savior he denied…
Heard the cheers of the crowd—when our Lord was crucified.

I have felt the pain of Judas—when the Savior he betrayed.
The cry of many hearts—when they laid Him in the grave.
I have heard the shouts of victory—He is risen indeed.
I knew He was from God—the true and righteous seed.

I have read in God's Word—The law of the letter…
That makes life worth living and the world much better.
Christ fulfilling the Law with Truth and Grace…
Finding God's Word—our resting place.

Now you can see some of the places I have been…
Traveling through this world amid darkness and sin.
Through the earth's clay and the written word.
My heart has understood and my ears have heard.

Nothing has ever been more profound.
No doctrine more sound
Than knowing how much God loves me…
When God became flesh so I could be free.

The past, present, future—God holds in His hand…
We can rest assured we are pilgrims in a foreign land.
God watches over His pure Word—His place of honor.
God is Love and the sky is our banner.

Learning about birth, life, death, and resurrection.
I have searched for wisdom in all of God's creation.
I have traveled many miles and seen many things
I have found God's Love in all that life brings.

RAINBOW:
And when they had found Him, they exclaimed: "Everyone is looking for You!"
Mark 1-37

GOD'S FAVOR

There is none righteous—not one on the earth.
Conceived in sin from the day of our birth.
We like sheep have gone astray.
Each of us to our very own way.

Our Father, the Creator from Heaven above.
Sent earth a Savior with Infinite Love.
The perfect image of the Father—is the Son.
In His seed, life's redemption was done.

In earth's garden was sinful soul of man.
God made Jesus overseer of the master plan.
He sent Him in flesh to feel our infirmity.
And give us His spiritual life for eternity.

God's throne room opened above the sky.
As angels sing, "Glory to God on High."
On earth peace and good will toward men.
The Savior was born to take away sin.

He was one with the Father's purity.
In His death—resurrection was a surety.
He is the great Shepherd of Love.
Born to lead His sheep to the Father above.

He was made sin for you and I…
So we could enter the throne room on high…
To have communion with our Father in prayer…
To find favor, love, discipline, and care.

Whosoever will may come and abide.
No one from their own sin can hide.
All of our sin was nailed to the cross.
It is "The Father's will," not one would be lost.

Sin is death—this we must see.
When we give it to God—we are set free.
Whosoever will may come in Jesus' name.
To break sin's bondages, fetters, shackles, and chains.

In God's Son we are never alone…
By His blood our sins are atoned.
He is called Savior, Lord, Master, and Friend.
Alpha, Omega, the beginning of no end.

RAINBOW:One generation will commend your works to another, they will tell of your mighty acts. They will speak of the glorious splendor of your wonderful works, and I will meditate on your wonderful works.
Psalms 145:4-5

GOD'S BEST

God has given us His best…
In the gift of His own Son.
He has given us the victory.
Many battles have been won.

Many bonds have been broken.
Many hearts have been healed.
Many lives have been changed…
Through the cross on Calvary's hill.

Many souls that were perishing…
From the hunger and thirst for God.
Have been fed the bread of Heaven…
From the seed—the Savior trod.

Many a wanderer, fugitive, and vagabond…
That has no earthly home…
Have been given God's blessings…
In the gift of God's own Son.

No one will ever know…
All the seeds that love has sown.
Through Jesus journey on the earth…
When God made flesh His home.

Because He came and dwelt among us…
And left us with hope.
Many a life has been strengthened…
With an everlasting cord of rope.

God has given us His best…
In the gift of His own Son.
He has given us a place of rest.
A place to call home.

RAINBOW:
Therefore, since we have a great high priest who has gone through the heavens, Jesus the Son of God, let us hold firmly to the faith we profess. For we do not have a high priest who is unable to sympathize with our weaknesses, but we have one who has been tempted in every way, just as we are, yet was with out sin.
Hebrews 4:14-15

GOD'S GREAT NATION

America was built on the foundation of God's Word...
With the right to choose the One whom we would serve.
"In God we trust" is written on our monetary means...
Tangible or intangible, seen or unseen.

Faith in God has brought us thus far...
To be the richest nation under the stars.
God as Creator of the whole universe...
Dispersing His blessing from nature's fallen curse.

Good overcomes evil—America believes.
Light overcomes darkness in nations that deceive.
Lift high the banner of freedom—let it now wave.
The Statue of Liberty is the home of the brave.

The Stars and the Stripes is a God-given seal...
Truth and light will win—evil and darkness will yield.
We believe in redemption, the cross, and the sword...
When one man stood firm on the foundation of God's Word.

One man conquered evil on Calvary's hill...
By His stars and stripes we are guided and sealed.
His blood cleanses us to make all things new...
The flag and the cross stand united and true.

Love overcame evil, death, and the darkness of hell…
Truth is our freedom—America!—stand strong and well.
The Lord is our refuge, our fortress, and our God…
He leads His children with His staff and His rod.

God's root is love—Love is His glory…
God's Holy Word was our Savior's life story.
The battle is finished where God resides…
Good comes out of evil—there is no place to hide.

RAINBOW:
If my people, who are called by my name, will humble themselves and pray and seek my face and turn from their wicked ways, then will I hear from heaven and will forgive their sin and will heal their land.
2 Chronicles 7:14

GOD'S TEMPLE

Jesus is—The Carpenter…
Who builds this house of clay.
He has given us His Spirit.
To live in it each day.

He has given us a promise…
That is steadfast and true…
That His Grace is sufficient…
In all we do.

He wants us to believe…
His works are of the righteous seed.
The pure love of God…
Who meets our every need.

God longs to feed us from the Master's table…
The All-Sufficient One—is willing and able.
Just a reminder—God owns it all.
The Bread He feeds us is not from the fall.

The Living Bread comes from our Father's throne…
He gives spiritual food to His very own.
More precious than silver and gold…
More than His earthly children can hold.

He created this house of clay…
And fashions the inside day by day.
He opens our spiritual eyes to see.
Heaven's bread coming from life's "Living Tree."

With His blood our sins are atoned.
He restores our souls for His very own.
God is the blood and seed donor.
Giving His children a place of great honor.

RAINBOW:
For other foundation can no man lay than that which is laid, which is Jesus Christ.
1 Corinthians 3:11

GOD'S LOVE ENDURES FOREVER

Love is the answer to all of our prayers.
Love is the reason we give and we share.
Love has it roots in our Savior the King.
Love is the reason for the church bells to ring.
Love is endowed by God, the Creator of Heaven and earth.
Love is the reason for our new spiritual birth.
God gave us the gift of perfect Love.
That reaches from earth to the Heavens above
Nowhere can you go that Love is not near.
Love overcomes darkness, deception, and fear.
Sadness, heartache, pain, weakness…
Sorrow, grief, burdens, despair, and sickness.
Each time we face temptation and sin…
God sees our Savior's blood and His Love will win.
Rooted, grounded, and established in Divine Love…
We are one with our Savior, who came from above.
Love conquered death, the wages of sin.
And opened death's tomb and let God's Light come in.
You see, whatever we suffer—whatever we face.
Love conquered the fall of the human race.
He has made us a promise so faithful and true…
Love will never mock, condemn, or forsake you.
He brings comfort, wisdom, and strength…
To those who are poor—to those who are weak.
So hold fast to the provision of your faith.
Love has no death—Love has no hate.

It all came together at the foot of "The Cross"…
When Love made the provision to pay sin's cost.
Now we are free in God's perfect Love…
From the cradle of birth—to the Heavens above.
Love one another is God's Divine Plan…
Love is the working of God's Holy hand.
In God's Infinite Love we live and abide.
There is no place on earth for sin to hide.
You see, God made us to be like Him…
Without darkness, deception, and sin.
When we walk by faith in God's Truth and Grace.
We are seated with Him in the heavenly place.
In His Kingdom of power, honor, and glory…
God poured out His Love in the birth of His story.
Love is the rise of nature's fall…
God is love and love conquers all.

RAINBOW:
For I am convinced that neither death, nor life, neither angels nor demons, neither the present nor the future, nor any powers, neither height nor depth, nor anything else in all creation, will be able to separate us from the love of God that is in Christ Jesus our Lord.
Romans 8: 38-39

GOD KNOWS AND UNDERSTANDS

There is not one burden that He does not bear.
There is not one pain that He does not share.
There is not one sin that He cannot forgive.
Out of the abundance of His life, we live.

God put it all in His Son's Holy Name.
His Love and His Word are always the same.
Giving us comfort in our times of sorrow.
The promise and hope of a better tomorrow.

No one can love us like our Savior…
God's special gift of His loving favor.
By His Spirit our spirit is fed.
In the path of His footprints our feet are led.

Not one tear He does not wipe away.
Not one hope will go astray.
Not one broken heart—He cannot heal.
Not anything hidden—He cannot reveal.

We face eternity with this in view.
In His Spirit our spirit is new.
God in us and by our side.
As the rise and fall of the eventide.

We walk not alone in the fall of human race.
We rise up in our Redeemer's Truth and Grace.
The light of the world never fades or dims.
We live, breathe, move, and have our being in Him.

This one truth God wants us to see.
In His Spirit—our spirit is set free.
We are all one in the universe.
God redeemed us from nature's fallen curse.

Suffering and pain is in all the earth, sea, and land.
God feels our infirmities—He understands.
As the early morning is covered with dew.
Out of our old nature—comes forth the new.

RAINBOW:
Yours, O Lord, is the greatness, and the power, and the glory, and the majesty, and the splendor, for everything in the heaven and in the earth is Yours. Yours, O Lord is the kingdom; you are exalted as head over all. Wealth and honor comes from you; you are ruler of all things. In your hands are strength and power to exalt and give strength to all. Now, our God, we give You thanks, and praise Your glorious name.
1 Chronicles 29:11-13

GOD OWNS IT ALL

There is no death or darkness in our Savior.
God gave us "The Gift" of His loving favor.
There is no sin in His pure Love.
Jesus brings good news from our Father above.

His word is all powerful—His Love is Divine.
His peace and joy is a gift of time.
His Grace is sufficient—His resurrection made known…
Through the old, rugged cross and the crown of thorns.

God gave us "The Gift" in His Holy name…
When he took our sin, guilt, disgrace, and shame.
He takes our burdens—He carries our load.
He shares Heaven's bread from the seed He sowed.

With His great Love of Light, Truth, and Grace.
No darkness or sin can we hide from His face.
Awake, O my soul!—God is the same.
He put all words in His Son's Holy Name.

God owns all that is good and all that is bad.
Joy and sorrow—hope and despair—happy and sad.
Faith and doubt—life and death—darkness and light.
He works it all together to give us spiritual sight.

We give Him all of our burdens and depend upon Him.
None is exempt from temptation, darkness, and sin.
His Grace is sufficient—His Truth is made known.
Through the old, rugged cross and the seed He has sown.

Wheat and tares—roses and thorns.
The tares He burns—the thorns He has worn.
The rose still blooms—the wheat is bread.
Where God's Love reigns – Jesus is head.

RAINBOW:
And we know that in all things God works for the good of those who love Him who have been called according to His purpose.
Romans 8:28

HOLY TRINITY

Living in a world of sin, darkness, and deception.
We need You, O Holy trinity…
To shine as a diamond in the rough.
Living in a world of anxiety, worry, and concerns.
We need You, O Holy Trinity…
To be our star shining in the darkness of our soul.
Living in a world of chaos and confusion.
We need You, O Holy Trinity…
To bring harmony, peace, and order.
Living in a world of doubts and fears.
We need You, O Holy Trinity…
To give us faith, hope, and love.
Living in a world of wars and disaster.
We need You, O Holy Trinity…
To shield us underneath the wings of Your spirit.
Living in a world of heartache, grief, sorrow, and pain.
We need You, O Holy Trinity…
To be our Truth, Grace, Shepherd, Conviction, and Guide.
Living in a world of uncertainty, insecurity, and instability.
We need You, O Holy Trinity.
To be our rock, our fortress, our stay.
In our valley of despair—midst the thorns and thistles.
We need You, O Holy Trinity…
To be our constant companion on earth.
Father Time and Mother Nature have taken their toll on our natural birth.
We need You, O Holy Trinity…

To carry us to our eternal home.
Your promises in "Jesus" have given us the gift of...
Faith, hope, and comfort; living in a fallen world.
Our earthly mortal flesh looks to Jesus.
The author and finisher of our faith.
O Holy Trinity, we need You.

RAINBOW:
The earth is the Lord's and the fullness thereof; the world, and they who dwell therein.
Psalms 24:1

HOPE

One white lily in the valley below…
One white lily with life all aglow.
One white lily blooms on a dark valley slope.
One white lily gives birth to hope.

One rose of Sharon crowned with thorns…
One rose mocked, scourged, and scorned.
One single rose gave birth to hope.
One rose forever blooms on nature's scope.

One bright morning star shone in the east…
One bright star for eyes to feast.
One bright star gave birth to hope.
One bright star helps humanity to cope.

On Calvary's hill stood one rugged cross…
One rugged cross stood for gain and loss.
One rugged cross gave hope to God's will.
One rugged cross stood on Calvary's hill.

One righteous seed born from above…
One righteous seed with roots of love.
One righteous seed gave birth to hope.
Faith—Hope—Love—Life's telescope.

RAINBOW:
For in this hope we were saved. But hope that is seen is no hope at all. Who hopes for what he already has? But if we hope for what we do not yet have, we wait for it patiently.
Romans 8:24-25

HOSANNA

Upon a lowly donkey…
Jesus rode one day.
Little children praised Him.
For He was God's way.

Hosanna—Hosanna!
Hosanna to the King.
Hosanna—Hosanna!
Little children sing.

Even today…
Little children say
Jesus is "The Truth."
Jesus is "The Way."

Hosanna—Hosanna!
Little children say…
Hosanna—Hosanna!
God loves us today.

Hosanna to the highest!
Hosanna to the King!
Save us! Lord Jesus.
All God's children sing.

RAINBOW:
The crowds that went ahead of Him and those that followed shouted. Hosanna to the Son of David! Blessed is He who comes in the name of the Lord! Hosanna in the highest!
Matthew 21:9

Dedicated to my grandchildren: Lauren, Jacob, Hannah, Walker, and Rebecca.

IF

If the beauty of Holiness…
Had not revealed…
The ugliness of sin…
We would not have known…
God's redemptive Love…
The Savior brought in.
If Jesus had not come…
Full of God's Glory…
Pages would never been written…
Of the Savior's life story.
If Jesus had not come…
Breathed His spirit—into the word…
Giving us victory through…
His righteous seed and pure blood.
If God had not sent…
His Son full of Truth and Grace…
To share in our sufferings…
And take sin's place…
All flesh born of earth…
Would never have heard…
The beauty of Holiness…
In God's Living Word.

No one would have felt...
God's purest of Love...
Had not the Savior...
Blotted out sin...
With His Holy blood.
No one would have known...
The difference God makes in human life...
If God had not sent His spirit...
In the God man...
To give us holiness...
In His redemptive plan.
To show us the way...
Back to our Father.
To give us hope...
For a greater tomorrow.
If God had not given Mary...
Salvation's song to sing.
There never would have been...
A church bell to ring...
Goodwill to men—Peace on earth...
If God had not given us...
The gift of a spiritual birth.

RAINBOW:
The sting of death is sin, and the power of sin is the law. But thanks be to God!
He gives us the victory through our Lord Jesus Christ.
1 Corinthians 15:56-57

ILLUMINATED LOVE

Out of the darkness there came a great light…
From the galaxies of stars that shine in the night.
God's promise to Abraham had been fulfilled…
Through the birth pain of suffering and Calvary's hill.

As many as the stars in the sky your children will be…
Gathered together as the sand in the sea.
Out of Father Time—eternity was born…
From the Cross of Calvary and a Crown of thorns.

Through man's flesh of struggle and strife…
Love conquered death and gave us new life.
Out of darkness, death, and despair…
LOVE—IS—BORN…
God cradled the world in His loving arms.

Trust in the Lord with all of your might.
Love rules the day and all through the night.
Count your blessings and magnify "The Lord"…
Our refuge—our strength—our shield—our sword.

Showers of blessings come from above…
Covering the earth with God's Infinite Love.
Gleaning God's truth from "The Living Word"…
From our fallen nature—GOD STILL SERVES!

RAINBOW:
When Jesus spoke again to the people. He said, "I am the light of the world. Whosoever follows me will never walk in darkness, but will have the light of life."
John 8:12

MOTHER

You left us a year ago, and oh the loss we felt.
The loss seemed more than I could bear.
On my knees I knelt.
The tears I shed for you.
I found I had new sight.
My heart belongs to Jesus.
There came a brand-new light.
Through those tears I shed for you…
My eyes were opened wide…
Within the light of Jesus—God the Father does abide.
Now I see your suffering was not at all in vain.
It was through nature's corruption you felt all those pains.

Now when I hear those words…
"My God, my God, why hast Thou forsaken me?"
I know without a doubt Jesus died for sin.
When He hung upon the tree,
Those words became an echo in my ears…
When I heard you cry through pain…
"My Jesus, don't You love me anymore?"
Then I remembered how Jesus suffered many years before.
Now I want the world to know just how I feel…
It was through your suffering, Mother…
That Jesus became real.

RAINBOW:
For I reckon that the sufferings of this present time are not worthy to be compared with the glory which shall be revealed in us.
Romans 8:18

In Memory of Mother
Alma Liles Crosby
March 2, 1898–January 9, 1975

Dedicated to my six siblings; Marie Price, Wilma Sharps, Paul Crosby, Laverne Norton, Jean Miller, Martyle Barwick

Mother was a pioneer. She was a character of strength, faith, honesty, devotion, determination, and hard work. She had a love for nature and the simply things of life. Mother, you carried us in your womb and in your heart. Today your spirit lives in our hearts. Through your suffering, pain, sorrows, and unspoken words, you left us a legacy of faith, hope, and love. Thank you.

IN PRAYER

With a crown of thorns…
The veil of darkness was torn…
I come boldly to "The Throne Room" in prayer.

With Jesus' blood, my sins are atoned…
God assures me I am His own…
In my "Mystical Garden" of prayer.

The Shepherd of Love has the way…
Of transforming my night to day…
When I enter my "Soul's Garden" in prayer.

He invites me in…
To "The Kingdom" of no end…
And my joy is unspeakable in prayer.

The travail of my soul…
Finds rest and is made whole…
On my knees in my "Trysting Place" of prayer.

No sin does abound…
There is glory all around…
In my "Beautiful Garden" of prayer.

Heaven prevails…
The Earth hails…
The time I spend with "The Savior" in prayer.

Holiness is there…
Nothing can compare…
When I commune with "God" in prayer.

In the gift of Christ's birth…
I join "The Most Holy" on earth…
When I unite with "The Lord" in prayer.

RAINBOW:
O thou who hearest prayer, unto thee shall all flesh come.
Psalm 65:2

IN PURSUIT OF GOD

Take all my sin, shame, and guilt away.
Keep me close, Lord, let me not go astray.
My burdens are too heavy to bear…
I need a trusted friend who will love me and care.

Crucify me, God, with the Savior.
That I, too, might find Your Love and favor.
Hide me in Your bosom of life.
Enjoying your peace without conflict and strife.

Mold me—make me—according to Your will.
Until my heart speaks "Peace be still"
Give me the faith to believe…
Your commandments and will to receive.

Help me to trust in Your Truth and Grace…
Sit at Your feet and look into Your face.
I might know that You are my Friend.
While I am seeking to find Your nail-scarred hand.

Deliver me from all doubts and fears..
Wipe away all my sadness and tears…
Lead me through this wilderness of sin…
With the light of Your Holy Spirit within.

I have sinned against You and You alone.
You are the Creator of my flesh and my bones.
Be my Guide, my Teacher, my soul's Lover.
In Your Spirit—I will serve others.

Help me to find rest in Your abiding place.
In the light of Your Truth and Grace.
This is the cry of my heart and mind.
More of Your Love as I pass through time.

Not my will—but Yours be done.
In the name of—The Father—The Spirit—The Son
O Eternal Father—everlasting throne.
My heart Your dwelling place—Heaven my home.

RAINBOW:
For whosoever findeth me, findeth life, and shall obtain favor of the Lord.
Proverbs 8:35

IT IS WRITTEN

When God came to earth in the midst of our sin.
He showed us the way to be spiritually like Him.
He nailed to the cross our sin, guilt, shame, and disgrace.
The fallen nature of the whole human race.

He created us in clay and the clay was marred.
We see the results in His hands that were scarred.
"The Potter" remolded the clay in His suffering and pain.
He redeemed the soul by His pure blood and Holy name.

God's Spirit is fruitful, faithful, and true.
For our sin-sick soul—He makes all things new.
With wings of faith—we are established in love.
Jesus, our righteousness, sends peace from above.

We live, breathe, and have our being in Him.
Where God is love and love has no end.
Seeing we are blessed far more than we know.
From the Son's Truth and Grace—we live and we grow.

A garment of righteousness—a garment of praise.
A crown of glory—for all of our days.
He gave us His Spirit of Grace, Truth, and Love.
Left us "The Love Letter" from our Father above.

A garment of salvation so pure and so white.
A light to guide us by day and by night
A wedding garment all spotless and pure.
The bride is waiting for the bridegroom to appear.

In clouds of great glory of joy, love, and peace…
Our battle will be over and our suffering will cease.
It is written that we might know…
Jesus' blood cleanses us whiter than snow.

RAINBOW:
But these are written that you may believe that Jesus is the Christ, the Son of God, and that believing you may have life in His name.
John 20:31

JESUS BE FORMED IN US

He came as a seed from the Father above.
He came full of grace, truth, peace, joy, and love.
Clothed in righteousness for humanity.
Opening the pathway to eternity.

God made Him lower than the angels above.
Crowned Him with glory and filled Him with love.
Power, blessing, and wisdom were in His hand.
The Living Word of Truth to rule the land.

Faith and God's Love was His passion and strife.
To conquer sin's death and give us new life.
We begin our journey at the foot of His cross.
Claiming God's spirit and the flesh as loss.

No one can love us like Jesus Christ, Our Lord.
His Word protects us—His shield and sword.
God cuts away the old to make room for the new.
Trust God's Word—the faithful and true.

Daily communion with the Father above
Forms us into His image of Love.
Travail in the old until all things are new.
Trust in the One who is faithful and true.

> Jesus goes with us every step of the way.
> He is our refuge—our strength—our stay.
> When we are lonely, fearful, and sad.
> He comforts, brings peace, and makes our heart glad.

RAINBOW:
My little children, of whom I travail in birth again until Christ be formed in you.
Galatians 4:19

Dedicated to all of God's earthly children.

JESUS IS LORD

Jesus is Lord of the Universe.
He holds all the power…
In the palm of His hand.
His Word is a double-edge sword,,,
Fulfilling the law of the land.
God sends the blessing of Heaven…
Through the spirit of His Son…
Grace that is all-sufficient…
His perfect will is done.

His is "The Kingdom"…
The power and the glory…
The sovereignty of God reigns…
In the pages of His story.
His truth is our freedom…
Pure Love is His heart…
His Word is "The Rock"…
That will never depart.

Message of the Father…
Through the Spirit of His Son…
Love and faithfulness met…
At the cross in perfect union…
Flesh and spirit joins…
In Holy communion.

Peace and righteousness kissed…
At the feet of the Savior…
Spiritual joy and bliss…
Through God's Love and favor…
Come, taste, and see…
Is the Master's call…
There is Love for one…
There is Love for all.

RAINBOW:
Love and faithfulness meet together; righteousness and peace kiss each other. Faithfulness springs forth from the earth, and righteousness looks down from heaven.
Psalms 85:10-11

KINGDOM WORKERS

Pray for workers…
For the Kingdom of God…
To gather and scatter the Seed…
The Redeemer has trod.

Pray for workers…
For God is the Kingdom…
The Power and Glory…
God breathed life into His Son's life story.

Pray for workers…
To come into agreement with the Word.
Many souls are saved…
When God's voice is heard.

Pray for workers…
Many souls lost could have been found.
Through the old, rugged cross…
Where God's doctrine is sound.

Pray for workers…
God's seed has been sown…
His blood fell to the ground…
Jesus the Redeemer—the name of renown.

Pray for workers…
For our families—loved ones—friends…
Need an abiding place…
From this world of temptation and sin.

Pray for workers…
To be fruitful, faithful, and true.
To God's blood covenant…
God created for me and for you.

RAINBOW:
Then He said to His disciples, "The harvest is plentiful but the workers are few. Ask the Lord of the harvest, therefore, to send out workers into His harvest field."
Matthew 9:37-38

KNOW THE ENEMY

Many times we fall, because we do not know
The seed of our flesh is our friend and our foe.
We struggle and strive with all our might.
And continue earth's journey with fear and a fight.

When we understand what God did for humanity…
His Spirit gives our hearts peace and our minds sanity.
Jesus opened the pathway to God's Kingdom of Love.
Giving us entrance into the Heavens above.

He gave us His character and His Holy name…
So we could walk on earth without fear and shame.
God's Word is our armor of living proof.
Our loins are girded with "The belt of truth."

We are children of the Kingdom—children of great Light.
His incorruptible Word wins the battles we fight.
Our home in the spirit is from our Father above.
The Creator of life—the Creator of Love.

In God's Holy Word is the love story of old.
Giving life's mystery to the mind, heart, and soul.
In God's Holy Word through His Holy pages…
Is the blueprint for life handed down through the ages.

Bread of Heaven and living water for the soul…
Comes from the Trinity with fire of pure gold.
Life is hid with God in His Son's love story.
For His is the Kingdom, the power, and the glory.

Taste and see in your humble supplication…
His mercy and truth continue to all generations.
There is life in His Spirit coming from Heaven's throne.
Through God's Living Word—His will is made known.

RAINBOW:
For our struggles is not against flesh and blood, but against the powers of this dark world and against the spiritual forces of evil in the heavenly realms.
Ephesians 6:12

LET IT BE

Let the beauty of Your Righteousness.
Fill my heart with Joy and Peace.
Let my thoughts and ways be Yours…
And Your Holiness never cease.

Let the mind of Christ be in me…
And His truth guide my ways.
Let all the darkness be dispersed…
And my heart filled with praise.

Let me count my every blessing…
Coming from the Father of Light.
Let the beauty of Your Holiness…
Give birth to my spiritual sight.

Let me be filled with Your presence.
And washed by Your Living Word.
Let every thought be taken captive…
To the Father's will above.

Let the glory of "The Son"…
Fill the earth, land, and sea.
Let Your Kingdom come to earth …
Through the cross of Calvary.

RAINBOW:
You are worthy, our Lord and God, to receive glory and honor and power; for you created all things by your will they were created and have their being."
Revelation 4:11

LETTER TO GOD

Dear God

I am sending you a letter…
I want to know You much better.
I want to know of Your Love and care.
And all my burdens You do bear.

I want to know the things You do…
To make all things good and true.
I want to feel Your joy and peace…
And drink from life's fountain that never cease.

I want to taste and see that the Lord is good…
And visit some of the places on earth He stood.
I want to smell the perfume so sweet…
That Mary poured upon His feet.

I long to look at the world through Your eyes…
And know the truth that makes one wise.
I yearn to touch the face of Your beloved…
And feel secure in His sinless blood.

I seek to find my rest in Thee…
And by Your truth my soul set free.
Forgive my unbelief is my prayer each day…
And never let me go astray…

Have the faith of my forefathers who toiled and labored…
To eat and drink from Your divine table
To hear the words of Your dear Son…
"Not my will but Thine be done."

Now I close this letter in humble supplication…
And thank You for Your invitation…
To come, taste and see.
The blessings that comes from Heaven's Trinity.

RAINBOW:
Pray all the time. Ask God for anything in line with the Holy spirit's wishes. Plead with him, reminding Him of your needs and keep paying earnestly for all Christians everywhere.
Ephesians 6:13

LOOKING WITHIN

Looking within—looking within…
Finding "The Savior" as my very best friend.
I was blind and I did not see…
Looking within I found I was free.
Looking within my heart and my mind…
Trusting my Friend—the Creator of time.
Finding living water in the garden of my soul…
Fire of love made from pure gold.
Looking within and finding deep love…
A solace of heart from the Heavens above.
Finding the way out of the darkness of night.
Finding great treasures of peace, joy, and light.
Looking up and looking within…
For "The Seed" of a baby born in Bethlehem.
Who lived His life so full and so free…
To open my spiritual eyes so I could see.
Healed my broken heart and set my spirit free.
He covered my heart with His Living Word.
The greatest love story I have ever heard.
Deep within the reservoir of my soul…
Is life's flowing waters and fire of pure gold.
Looking without I could not see…
When I looked within—I found I was free.
Each individual has a world of their own…
A great garden of life where seeds are sown.

Some good and some evil with a light to expose…
The darkness within so everyone knows…
To follow the light so the world can see…
That God's Love can set each heart free.
Looking within—we find a friend…
To help us through this wilderness of sin…
To lighten our burdens and carry our load…
From the troubles and sorrows of seeds we sow.
Looking without we cannot see…
It's looking within that sets our hearts free.
To find within the pages of one's soul…
A city where streets are paved with pure gold.
Looking without—looking within…
Finding a heart full of love for a soul full of sin.
Finding joy and sorrow of living on earth…
Between the two Adams that gave us this birth.

RAINBOW:
The heart is deceitful above all things and beyond cure. Who can understand it? "I the Lord search the heart and examine the mind, to reward a man according to his conduct, according to what his deeds deserve."
Jeremiah 17: 9-10

LOVE'S RESTING PLACE

Love finds its resting place…
In the heart of the Most High.
A reservoir of living water…
For the earth, land, sea, and sky.

In the mystery of God's Kingdom…
There is a vast supply.
It covers the universe…
A well that never runs dry.

God's Spirit redeemed the earth…
In His Son's righteous seed.
For the lowly, weary, pilgrim…
He wills to supply our every need.

We travel through the earth…
In a dry and barren land.
The thirsty soul looks up by faith…
To the "Great I Am."

He guides each star…
He directs each plan.
He holds the universe…
In the palm of His Holy hands.

Who can know the Love of God?
Who can know His Name?
Only the Son who left His footprints…
In earth's sorrows, grief, and pain.

Love bears the fruit of God's Holy Spirit.
The scars are in His feet and hands…
His pierced side and broken heart.
Joined flesh to spirit in God's redemptive plan.

RAINBOW:
Arise, shine, for your light has come, and the glory of the Lord rises upon you.
Isaiah 60:1

LOVE REIGNS

God reigns in joy, peace, and righteousness.
God reigns in mercy, forgiveness, and faithfulness.
In Truth and Grace—God's Love has no end.
Love is our true and faithful friend.

Love understands the nature of fallen things.
God still rules and Love still reigns.
God gave all—to set our spirit free.
Love reigns in you—love reigns in me.

God clothed us in His righteousness.
Feeds us with power, wisdom, and faithfulness.
He took the place of sin, guilt, and shame.
And leads us by His Holy Name.

God's blood was shed to make us new.
Never more our sin to view.
He took our fleshly ego to the grave.
God pardons—sin's debt was paid.

God's Word is Truth—Truth cannot lie.
Mocked, betrayed, denied, ridiculed, tested, and tried.
With a broken heart and nail-pierced hands—Love calls.
God is love and love conquers all.

RAINBOW:
This is love: not that we loved God: but that He loved us and sent His Son as an atoning sacrifice for our sins.
1 John 4:10

MORE LIKE JESUS

The less I have of the self in me.
The more like Jesus I will be.
It was His cross, His blood, and His seed
That pardoned my sins and set my soul free.

Free from the world, the flesh, and sin.
Jesus' life blood brought redemption in.
He paved the way back to our Creator.
To become our intercessor and mediator.

All of our iniquities were placed on Him…
To set us free from the temptation of sin.
His is The Kingdom—The power—The Glory…
And the reason for the Christmas story.

It is not a myth—but a legend so true.
History records this time of review.
The symbol of hope while we live on earth…
When God became man through a virgin's birth.

He became poor, as poor as can be…
When He clothed Himself in humanity.
He became the poorest in this world below.
So the riches of Heaven He could bestow.

Showers of blessing that ears have never heard…
All from the gift of God's Living Word.
This is "The Truth" that sets the flesh free.
More like Jesus and less like me.

Sitting with God on the right side of His throne…
With the earth as His footstool and Heaven His home.
All power and authority has been given to Him.
Our Redeemer, our Savior, our Lord, our Friend.

RAINBOW:
He must become greater: I must become less.
John 3:30

MY EVERYTHING

God supplies all of my needs…
From His Son's righteous seed.
His blood I know…
Washes me whiter than snow.
He is everything to me.

In my joy and in my sorrow…
In every day and every tomorrow.
In peace and despair…
He is always there.
He is everything to me.

In my suffering and in my pain…
God's Love is always the same.
In death and in destruction…
There is hope and resurrection.
He is everything to me.

Jesus was cradled in God's Love
Came to earth from Heaven above.
He is in the great and in the small…
He is "The Word," He is my all.
He is everything to me.

In depth and in height…
In length and in width…
His Love surpasses land and sea…
He rules my heart in righteousness.
He is everything to me.

Power, Glory, Honor, and King…
Majestic, Splendor, Riches Supreme.
Heaven crowned His death on the cross…
When Jesus paid sin's cost.
He is everything to me.

Through His blood and righteous seed…
By His faith my heart believes.
God's only Son had no sin…
From the beginning to end.
He is my everything.

RAINBOW:
Christ also suffered. He died once for the sins of all us guilty sinners, although He Himself was innocent of any sin at any time, that He might bring us safely home to God.
1 Peter 3:18

MY FATHER'S CHILD

I am my Heavenly Father's child…
He brings me joy and makes my heart smile.
In all my ways I acknowledge Him…
As my Master, Redeemer, Savior, and Friend.

I abide in Him and He abides in me…
In His Spirit—my spirit is free.
Free from all burdens, cares, and concerns…
In God's Love, the Light infinitely burns.

Living in this world below the Heavens…
His Truth and Grace is Love without leaven.
I sought His Truth with all of my heart…
I found God's love gift will never depart.

I am walking and talking daily with Him…
My forever Love—my constant Friend.
No more will I walk in the darkness of night…
He gave me His Love of Eternal Light.

He promised never to leave me alone…
His Love will be my eternal home.
Now I am walking free with Him by my side…
He is my Teacher, my Comforter, my Guide.

He bids His children to walk in His righteousness…
So we won't walk alone in sin's darkness.
Following Him will lead us to our eternal home…
Where pain and suffering will never more roam.

Our sin, guilt, and shame He bore at Calvary…
So God could be in you and God could be in me.
His suffering was not at all in vain…
It was Heaven's Love for fallen earth to claim.

Stay close and cleave to the Son of Truth and Grace…
The One God sent to take sin's place.
Our forever Love and constant Friend He will be.
The Creator of Life, Love, and Liberty.

RAINBOW:
Then the godly shall shine as the sun in their Father's kingdom. Let those with ears, Listen!
Matthew 13:43

NEVER ALONE

When you feel sad, rejected, and alone.
On this earth, there is no place you can call home.
When you feel your burdens are too heavy to bear.
You have this feeling that no one really cares.

When you feel betrayed, denied, and forsaken.
When you feel like your heart is breaking.
When you feel grief, pain, suffering, and loss.
This is the reason we reflect on the cross.

God in His infinite wisdom from above.
Has cradled us in His everlasting Love.
Heaven is our home—the earth is our loss.
God joined earth to Heaven at the foot of the cross.

When you feel all of these emotions from living on earth
Reflect on the story of Jesus and His birth.
No one can love you so faithful and true.
Your heart is God's heart, too.

The great Shepherd will never lead you astray.
He will feed you fresh manna from Heaven each day.
Each morning take time to spend with Him.
His way is narrow, but His light never dims.

Many a trial, suffering, pain, and tribulation.
God took care of it in His Son's resurrection.
Your spiritual journey begins at the foot of the cross.
Stay close and cleave and count your suffering as loss.

There waits for you a brighter tomorrow…
Where there is no grief, pain, or sorrow.
God prepared a way to our heavenly home.
So remember, my child, you are never alone.

RAINBOW:
Stay away from the love of money; be satisfied with what you have. For God has said, "I will never, never fail you nor forsake you." That is why we can say without any doubt or fear, "The Lord is my Helper and I am not afraid of anything that mere man can do to me."
Hebrews 13: 5-6

NEW BEGINNINGS

Every day is a new beginning...
In the earth, land, and sea.
Every day is a new beginning...
There is no end—there is eternity.

What we begin today...
Let it be for everyone's good.
There is no tomorrow...
Only man has misunderstood.

God has put no end to our learning...
About the Heavens and the earth.
Every day is a new beginning...
Bringing forth new birth.

What we sow upon the earth...
The angels in Heaven will reap.
Separating the thorns from the roses...
The tares from the wheat.

Roses and thorns—tares and wheat.
What we sow is—what we reap.
Among the thorns—there is the rose.
Among the tares—there is the wheat.

In all our chaos and confusion...
There is the Word of God.
Who built eternity's foundation...
From the seed our Savior trod.

God's Kingdom was completed...
On the day that Jesus died.
From His seed of righteousness...
The world was crucified.

There will be no thorns or tares.
The wheat and roses will bloom.
Eternity has no death.
Death has no tomb.

RAINBOW:
And the one sitting on the throne said, "See, I am making all things new! And then he said to me. "Write this down, for what I tell you is trustworthy and true: It is finished! I am the A and Z the beginning and the End. I will give to the thirsty the springs of water of life—as a gift."
Revelation 21:5-6

NUMBERED AND NAMED

How precious are your thoughts of me.
How great and how high…
Numbered by the sand of the sea…
And the stars in the sky.

You spoke and the worlds were framed.
You said, "Let it be" and there was light…
Watching your creation change—you remain the same.
Your words divided the day from the night.

Your thoughts and ways are not my own…
They are pure, true, and holy.
My sin is made known…
From Your Love of Truth and Glory.

You know the words that I speak…
And my thoughts from afar.
You bless the poor, lowly, humble, and meek.
And know the names and number of each star.

You knew me before I was conceived in sin.
You sheltered me underneath Your wings.
You know my goings out and comings in,
"Salvation's song" You gave me to sing.

You possess me in my inward parts.
And covered me in my mother's womb.
You cradled me in sin's darkness.
And opened the grave to death's tomb.

Your thoughts are—Love made known.
In the words of Your only Begotten Son…
Where the eternal Kingdom of Life was sown.
Finished—completed—immaculately done.

The body of Your church gives light and hope.
To a world who sits in darkness…
Its power and strength helps us to cope.
As we seek Your Love and righteousness.

Such knowledge is too high for me…
Yet, I am fearfully and wonderfully made.
Your Love for my soul—made my salvation free…
With the blood of Your Son—my sin debt is paid.

RAINBOW:
Psalms 139

OH GLORIOUS DAWNING

Oh glorious dawning—this wonderful day.
Jesus our Savior in constant array.
His peace in us will forever abide.
His presence surrounds us—in Him we hide.

Oh, glorious dawning—this wonderful day.
Jesus is forever our rock and our stay.
Whatever befalls us—whatever may come.
His Kingdom is forever—His Will be done.

His is the Kingdom, the Power, and the Glory.
Eternity is written in Jesus' life story.
The earth is His footstool—Heaven is His throne.
We are rooted in His Love—the place we call home.

The Author and Finisher of faith that abounds.
We are standing with Him on holy ground.
In following Him—we climb higher each day.
He is—the truth—the life—the way.

Back to His Father and our Father He goes.
His Holy Spirit on us He bestows.
All earthly ground is sinking sand.
The Living Word of our Father—will forever stand.

Today, we will eat fresh bread from Heaven.
Pure, true, faithful, and unleavened.
Today, we are seated with Jesus on high.
Receiving God's Truth and Grace that will never die.

Jesus gave us the invitation to come, taste, and see.
The truth that sets our hearts and minds free.
So all you that are burdened down with care.
Come, taste and see—God's Love is everywhere.

Come and see—Go and tell.
The invitation and commission—learn it well.
For many are sinking in a sea of despair
We must tell them of God's Love and tender care.

RAINBOW:
A glorious throne exalted from the beginning, is the place of our sanctuary.
Jeremiah 17:12

Taste and see that the Lord is good; blessed is the man who takes refuge in Him.
Psalms 34:8

OLD THINGS

All earthly things that lead us astray.
All of our thoughts and all of our ways.
All of our pain, suffering, grief, and sorrow.
All of our yesterday's and tomorrows.

All of our heartaches, trials, and tribulations.
All of our troubles, chaos, and confusion.
All of our doubts and all of our fears.
All of our sadness and all of our tears.

All famine, poverty, sickness, and disease.
All human fame, riches, power, and prestige.
All thorns, thistles, flowers, and trees.
All that is born of the corruptible seed.

In all of Heaven and all of the earth.
Jesus' blood gives us a new birth.
Only His Word so pure and so true.
Will come forth to make all things new.

The mind of Christ and the heart of God.
Created the righteous seed the Savior trod.
They fashioned together this great redemptive plan.
Jesus would become—The Word—The flesh–The Man.

Old things have passed away—all things are new.
The promise in "The Word" so faithful and true.
Mortality and corruption shall decease.
We will go out with joy—be led forth with peace.

As heavens are higher than the earth.
So is the newness of our spiritual birth.
God's thoughts and ways are higher than ours.
Fulfilling earth's law with love's greatest power.

Culminating together—to give us "The Word."
The beauty of Holiness—His Spirit to serve.
Eternal blessing—bread without leaven.
Pure wine to drink from the portals of Heaven.

RAINBOW:
Therefore, if any man be in Christ, he is a new creation; the old has gone, the new will come!
2 Corinthians 5:17

ONE

That we might be one was our Savior's prayer.
One with the Creator—in His Love and tender care.
One in the Heavens in His Spirit Divine.
One in the earth in His fullness of time.

One in His suffering of living on earth.
One with His Son, who gave us a new birth.
One in His Name filled with His Glory.
To grow in "The Word" of His living story.

One with nature—one with our Father.
One who loves us like no other.
One who can lead us in the pathway of light.
One who dispels the darkness of night.

Forgave all of our debts and all of our debtors.
Breaking our bondage, chains, and fetters.
What an honor to walk in His Truth and Grace.
The privilege to sit with Him in His heavenly place.

One in His righteousness, peace, joy, and love.
Cleansed from our sin by His spotless blood.
Filled with His Spirit—crowned with His glory.
So we could call God, our Father, holy.

One who gave us the Kingdom of God.
Leads us in green pastures by His staff and His rod.
In the fullness of His wisdom, honor, and glory.
God shares His love through the Savior's life story.

One to be thankful for God's Love in me.
One to bow before Him on bended knees.
One to worship and praise His Holy Name.
Glorify Him in suffering, in trials, and in pain.

RAINBOW:
My prayer is not for them alone. I pray also for those who will believe in Me through their message, that all of them may be one. Father, just as you are in me and I am in you. May they also be in us so that the world may believe that you have sent me. I have given them the glory that you gave me, that they may be one as we are one. I in them and you in me.
John 17:20-22

ONE DAY AT A TIME

Walking with Jesus one day at a time.
Leaving the old things of yesterday behind.
Feeding on His spirit of Love Divine.
Eating fresh bread and drinking new wine.

Passing through earth—one day at a time.
Filling our hearts with God's Love Divine.
Building ourselves up in the most Holy faith.
For the Love and the Truth of Jesus' namesake.

More precious than silver or gold.
Is the blessing of Heaven—the wealth of the soul.
The Eternal Kingdom God prepared for us…
The day that He died and took nature's curse.

The gift of God passed down through the ages.
Written in blood through—the Word's Holy Pages.
Gleaning the fields full of stubble and hay.
Finding Love in God's Spirit day by day.

The Word is living and none can compare.
The life in His Spirit He gave us to share.
The Truth and the Grace—in the gift of His Son.
For His Will and His Way on earth to be done.

The way of the flesh is sinking sand.
God pours out His Spirit through the heart of man.
To be shed abroad in our hearts each day.
Lighting the world to God's pathway.

"Come unto Me" all that are laden down with care.
Is the call of the Master in the cross we bear.
"My yoke is easy and my burden is light."
God leads His children in the pathway of right.

The Spirit is the path that leads to our eternal home.
God, who loves and cares for us, is still on His throne.
He bids us to come to Him through the blood of His Son.
Adorned as His bride—the Bridegroom says, "Come."

RAINBOW:
The spirit and the bride say, "Come!" and let him who hears say, "Come! Whoever is thirsty, let him come: and whoever wishes, let him take the free gift of the water of life."
Revelation 22:17

OUR DWELLING PLACE IN GOD

Some people say we live on earth amid sickness and sin.
God's children have a better place, since Jesus came in.
We live in God—the most Holy place.
He lives in us with Truth and Grace.
We live and breathe and have our being in Him.
Where there is no darkness—no death—no sin.

You see, we are deceived if we believe otherwise.
God anointed Jesus' Spirit and He opened our eyes.
The mystery of God's truth—Jesus taught us.
We became God's children when He took our curse.
No evil or lies can come near the door of our heart.
God's Grace and Truth will never depart.

We all have this battle of life called flesh and sin.
Abiding in Jesus—the light will never dim.
God rules and reigns in our hearts with Love.
We are looking to Jesus from the Heavens above.
He is the Author and Finisher of our faith in God.
He created new life in us with His very own blood.

When you are lonely, discouraged, and sad.
Remember God owns it all and be very glad.
We have exchanged our old nature of sin for the new.
We are in Christ—the faithful and true.
Study God's word and learn how to pray.
Grow in Grace and Truth—a little each day.

Soon you will know the mystery of life.
Where God is Love with no struggle or strife.
Each day we eat Heaven's bread and drink the new wine.
We live in God's Kingdom of Love all the time.
Surrounded by joy, peace, light, truth, and grace.
We will never want to leave this beautiful place.

God came to earth to secure our salvation in Him.
Jesus–the Righteous Seed—born in Bethlehem.
Emanuel—"God with us" in His visit to earth.
In Him we are baptized in a new spiritual birth.
Old things of the fleshly nature have passed away.
Jesus is our Refuge—Our rock—Our stay.

Count your blessings each day you live on earth.
We are abiding in Jesus, who gave us God's birth.
God's Love is a gift where we live each day.
Not life—not death—can take it away.

RAINBOW:
As the Father has loved me, so have I loved you. Now remain in my love.
John 15:9

JESUS

You were crucified to the world…
The world was crucified unto you.
The Son of God—the son of man…
Faithful—pure—sincere—true.

You are exalted above all…
You raised us up from Nature's fall.
We live—breathe—and move in you.
Each day Your Spirit brings forth the new.

You clothed us in Your righteousness…
And crowned us with Your glory…
And gave us Your Spirit.
Where all things are Holy.

Your flesh is Heaven's bread…
Your blood is new wine.
You seat us at God's table…
With His pure love divine.

You opened "The Door"…
That no man can close.
You gathered the thorns and thistles…
And left us "The Rose."

You gave us Your Holy Spirit…
And taught us to love.
You revealed God's truth…
From the Heaven's above.

You are to be magnified…
We are to be sanctified.
You are to be glorified…
We are to be crucified.

Until the old wineskins become new…
We feed off your righteousness
The Faithful—The True.

RAINBOW:
The Jesus used this Illustration: "No one tears off a piece of new garment to make a patch for an old one.Not only will the new garment be ruined, but the new garment will look worse with a new patch on it! And no one puts new wine into the old wineskins, for the new wine bursts the old skins, ruining the skins and spilling the wine. New wine must be put into new wineskins. But no one after drinking the old wine seems to want the fresh and the new. The old ways are best, they say."
Luke 5:36-39

PRAYER TO THE SURGEON

Open my eyes, Lord—that I might see.
Open my heart—to Your purity.
Open my thoughts—to Your perfect Word.
Open my ears—to things unheard.

To the Gospel of peace—let my feet be shod.
My allegiance, faithfulness, and loyalty to God.
Set the light of your glory on my face.
Stop all flesh from taking your place.

Open my soul—to the garden of love…
To the tree of life that is rooted above.
Wash me in Your blood—that flowed from Your veins.
Across the ocean divide and the earth's great plane.

Open my flesh—so the spirit can see…
The surgeon's hands that crucify the self in me.
In Jesus' perfect Love, peace, and serenity..
Now and forever through eternity.

Sit me at Your table of Love Divine…
To eat Your bread and drink Your wine.
Forever and always—abide in my heart…
From the light of the day and the midnight dark.

This request to the Surgeon, I pray.
Will shed your light on the narrow way.
So others can see…
Jesus is the way to eternity.

RAINBOW:
May peace and blessings be yours from God the Father and our Lord Jesus Christ. He died for our sins just as God our Father planned, and rescued us from this evil world in which we live. All glory to God through all the ages of eternity.
Galatians 1:3-5

REDEEMED

God's Love in His Holy Spirit…
Is "The Gift" within His Son.
He has given us His life…
Where great victory has been won.

He has given us access…
To His throne room on high.
Through His blood of redemption.
We can reach beyond the sky.

He has given us a place to rest…
He has given us a place to heal…
He has given us a place of refuge…
If we surrender to His Will.

God has not given us a spirit of fear…
But power of pure Love…
Through "The Cross" of Christ…
Comes inward blessing from above.

There is power for every hour.
There is light within the soul.
There is fellowship with "The Father."
Through "The Cross" we are made whole.

We can boldly come to our Father's throne…
Through the blood of "The Anointed One."
Ask for mercy, grace, and forgiveness…
For the wrong we have done.

His Grace is sufficient.
His Love will endure.
God stands upon His promises.
They are steadfast and sure.

RAINBOW:
Let us then approach the throne of grace with confidence, so that we may receive mercy and find grace to help us in our time of need.
Hebrews 4:16

REDEMPTION

Rest for the weary.
Comfort for the sorrow.
Bread for the hungry.
Eternity for tomorrow.

Life for the dead.
Light for darkness.
Hope for despair.
Nothing can compare.

Faith for our doubts.
Health for our sickness.
Peace for our fears.
Strength for our weakness.

The Spirit for our flesh.
Heaven for our home.
Victory for the defeated.
Never more to roam.

Riches for rags.
Wisdom for our foolishness.
Glory for our crown.
Joy for our sadness,

Come unto Me.
Is the Savior's call.
Jesus, our Creator.
God is in all.

Clothed in His righteousness.
Crowned with His Glory.
Fed by His Spirit.
Victory in His story.

Everything points to Jesus.
No matter where we roam.
The Author and Finisher of our faith.
Eternity—our home.

RAINBOW:
Glorify the Lord with me; let us exalt His name together.
Psalms 34:3

ROOTS AND WINGS

Jesus, the seed of righteousness…
Still lives on earth in Truth and Grace.
With roots of love and wings of faith.
We are free to soar to the heavenly place.

He feeds us the bread of Heaven…
As we walk by faith in Him.
The way is straight and narrow…
But the light never dims.

God planted His righteous seed…
Into the heart of the earth among sinful man.
To separate the shaft from the wheat…
Giving voice to the "Great I Am."

Build your faith on God's infallible Word.
Spread the message of hope far and wide.
The seed planted on earth has resurrected..
Back to our Father's side.

The cross is the symbol of resurrection.
God's Love created the redemptive plan.
Giving birth to faith, hope, and love…
In the heart and soul of man.

He gives us an invitation…
To come, taste, and see.
God's sacrificial Love from Heaven.
For fallen humanity.

The tree of life has all God's fruits…
To live life in harmony.
Righteousness, peace, and joy…
The promise of eternity.

There is no limitation or law.
When the heart is established in love.
Grace and Truth set the spirit free.
God's message to earth from the Heavens above.

Heaven and earth—cross and crown.
Love and faith—roots and wings.
Truth and Grace—joy and peace.
Lord of lords—King of kings.

RAINBOW:
So do not fear, for I am with you; do not be dismayed, for I am your God. I will strengthen you, and help you; I will uphold you with my righteous right hand.
Isaiah 41:10

SACRIFICE OF PRAISE

Praise the Lord, O my soul…
Where the living water of life still flows.
The pure bread unleavened…
Coming down from the portals of Heaven.

Praise the Lord for love not tainted with sin…
And the light from Heaven never grows dim.
No death, nor scavengers can be found…
Where bands of angels and glory abound.

Praise the Lord for His Truth and Grace…
A gift that encircled the whole human race.
Not death, nor life can take it away…
Forever, our rock, our fortress, our stay.

Praise the Lord in trials and tribulation…
Through suffering and pain—God planned our salvation.
What waits for us is more precious than gold…
This is God's love story from the pages of old.

Praise the Lord for time spent on earth…
When God gave man a new spiritual birth.
Where faith, hope, and love is life's expectation…
In the fullness of time—waits joy and celebration.

Praise Him in the morning for His loving kindness…
Praise Him in the night for His faithfulness.
God invites earth's children to come and dine…
He encourages the praise of His people all the time.

Praise Him in the valley and on the mountain high…
Until our praise reaches far above the sky.
All life in the ocean, land, earth, and sea…
Sing songs of praise—Heaven is our destiny.

RAINBOW:
Through Jesus, therefore, let us continually offer to God a sacrifice of praise—the fruit of lips that confess His name.
Hebrews 13:15

It is good to praise the Lord and make music to your name, O Most High, to proclaim your love in the morning and your faithfulness at night.
Psalms 92:1

SALVATION'S SONG

All I know and all I see...
Is God's Love for you and me.
Jesus gave His life to set us free.
On the cross of Calvary.
He took our sin, guilt, shame, and disgrace...
Redeemed us by taking our place.

All our sorrows, grief, hurt, and pain...
His cross was our eternal gain.
God's Love for us is all I see...
He won life's battle for eternity.
Just one drop of his Holy blood...
Has covered us with His blanket of Love.

I know that our Redeemer lives...
To our spirit He gives and gives.
In exchange for our flesh of lust and pride...
His Spirit of Grace and Truth abide.
Joy unspeakable and full of glory...
The Love of God reigns in Jesus' story.

In our hearts always to stay...
Not death, nor life, can take it away.
Unconquerable Love, Truth, and Grace.
When the Savior of Love took sin's place.
Joy to the world and peace on earth...
The greatest love story is the Savior's birth.

Let not your heart be troubled, nor afraid.
In Jesus' death the righteous are saved.
In all I know and all I see...
God still gives a song of victory.
Peace on earth and good will to men....
God's love story sung over again and again.

RAINBOW:
And Mary said, My soul doth magnify the Lord, and my spirit hath rejoiced in God my Savior.
Luke 1:46-47

SALVATION

God has given us an invitation…
To come, drink, eat, and dine.
The bread of life and living water…
Where there is plenty all the time.

God shares the Glory of His Son…
That has never been denied.
His Kingdom was completed…
The day He was crucified.

Our body is the temple…
Of God's Love, Truth, and Grace.
It has no place for evil…
For God's Son took evil's place.

He walked the straight and narrow…
The path of faith He trod.
To lead us in green pastures…
By His staff and by His rod.

There can be no evil…
Come near the door of our heart.
His Word is God's Truth…
His Grace can never depart.

His blood covered the earth…
It was God's redemptive plan.
To secure our salvation…
By the works of His Holy hand.

He has clothed us in His righteousness…
He has crowned us with His Glory…
He has sealed us by His Spirit…
And we cry, Holy, Holy, Holy.

RAINBOW:
And they were calling to one another: "Holy, Holy, Holy is the Lord Almighty; the whole earth is full of His glory."
Isaiah 6:3

SET FREE

There is no darkness in our Savior.
There is no sin in His pure Love.
There is no death in His Spirit.
Only "The Truth" from the Heavens above.

His body—His blood—His Word—His cross.
Filled all the law and the prophets of old.
His is—the Kingdom—the Power—the Glory.
The greatest love story ever told.

God took the seed of the Savior…
Bringing life out of death trough His Love.
Dispelling all darkness of sin.
Covering the earth with His blood.

Angels carried this message from Heaven.
There's forgiveness and mercy for all.
Come unto Him, all you weary and heavy laden.
He has raised us from nature's fall.

Earth and Heaven were given to Him.
All glory, honor, praise, and thanksgiving.
He broke the law of sin and death.
His Spirit is all life-giving.

The Lamb overcame earth's sin and darkness.
We overcome by the blood of the Lamb.
In His Spirit is life that is worth living.
We have been set free by "The Great I Am."

All things belong to Him.
All creatures great and small.
In all the Heavens, earth, sea, and land.
We find God's Love is the greatest of all.

We cannot live without His life-giving Spirit.
His truth still marches on.
Earth is our temporal dwelling place.
Heaven is our eternal home.

RAINBOW:
Therefore, there is now no condemnation for those who are in Christ Jesus, because through Christ Jesus the law of the Spirit of life set me free from the law of sin and death.
Romans 8:1-2

SHEPHERD OF THE KINGDOM

In the Kingdom of God's Love.
Jesus declared all things new.
He begins each day…
As the early morning's dew.

Jesus is Lord—He cannot lie…
He is constant, just, and fair…
His Truth gives us liberty…
There is no other who can compare.

Jesus is nature's Redeemer…
Let us grow in His Truth and Grace.
One day we shall see "The righteous One"…
With all of God's Glory on His face.

Jesus' Kingdom rules the heavens and earth…
Let all eyes be placed on Him.
Jesus, the Great Shepherd of Love…
Jesus, our constant Friend.

Be still, listen, and know…
When you are lonely, rejected, and sad…
Jesus is the very best Friend…
The human heart has ever had.

You are never alone in this fleshly world.
God who is love—owns it all.
He gives mercy, truth, forgiveness, and grace…
Jesus redeemed us from nature's fall.

Faith in God's Kingdom, we must never deny…
As we grow in the gift of His righteous seed.
Jesus is the Way, the Truth, the Life…
He supplies all of earth's need.

Be faithful, thankful, and praise Him…
In all earth's sorrow and pain.
Count all things of earth as loss…
The Kingdom of God as our gain.

RAINBOW:
Jesus went throughout Galilee, teaching in their synagogue, preaching the good news of the Kingdom, and healing every disease and sickness among the people.
Matthew 4:23

SOMETIMES

Sometimes I am lonely—sometimes I am sad.
Sometimes I am fearful—sometimes I am glad.
Sometimes there is sorrow and pain I must bear.
Sometimes it feels like no one cares.

Sometimes I am discouraged—laboring with fear.
Sometimes in hope—sometimes in despair.
Searching and seeking for places unknown.
For arms that will hold me when I feel alone.

Sometimes I carry life's burdens and grief.
Having faith in Jesus' cross, I find my relief.
Sometimes I am frightened in all that I see.
Then I am grateful for God's life-giving tree.

Toiling and laboring in this world below.
With God's mercy, goodness, and grace He bestows.
When my soul is cast down then I look above.
Thankful to Jesus for His Kingdom of Love.

Focusing on Jesus—God's redemptive seed.
Who carries my burdens and meets my need.
His Grace is sufficient—His Love will endure.
His blood gives new life—I feel secure.

Than I am thankful for my journey on earth.
Thankful for God, who gave me two births.
Thankful His Word will endure to the end.
In the gift of His Son—my uppermost Friend.

RAINBOW:
In Him we have redemption through His blood, the forgiveness of sins, in accordance with the riches of God's grace that He lavished on us with all wisdom and understanding.
Ephesians 1:7-8

LORD OVER ALL

The Lord joined together…
The old to make new.
At the foot of the cross…
With Heaven in view.

His name is exalted…
Year after year.
While some live in Hope
And some live in despair.

Some live in Truth…
While some live in deception.
Some live in Peace and Joy…
Through the earth's resurrection.

Some live in "The Spirit"…
So full and so free.
Some live in the flesh…
Where they are deceived.

Some live by faith…
Some live by fear.
Some live between…
Hope and despair.

Some live with…
Suspicion, animosity and greed.
Far away from God's gift…
Of The Son's righteous seed.

Some are rooted and grounded…
In God's Great love.
With confidence and assurance…
In "The Seed" and "The Blood."

Always keeping their eyes…
Focused on Him.
Who conquered "The Fall"…
And walked among men.

RAINBOW:
One God and Father of all, who is above all, and through all, and in you all.
Ephesians 4:6

TAKING THE RISK

Taking the risk of walking by faith.
Overcoming the darkness of night.
Taking the risk of loving God.
Walking in His brightness of light.

Taking God's hand with confidence.
That there is no darkness at all.
Thanking our Savior for His Divine Love.
That delivered us from nature's fall.

Taking the risk of walking by faith.
Holding to God's changeless Word.
Taking the risk of loving the enemy.
And finding great joy when we serve.

Taking the risk of loving and serving.
And forget not the price Jesus paid.
To redeem our sin-sick soul.
When He overcame sin, death, and the grave.

Taking the risk to walk in the light.
And surrender your will to God's Infinite Love.
Trusting in His Kingdom of Truth and Grace.
To bring us to the Heavens above.

Taking the risk of being loved…
By the true and faithful One.
Taking the risk of believing the truth.
The words spoken by God's own son.

With the blood, the seed of God's Immaculate Love.
And the offering of His nail-scarred hands.
He reached down from the Heavens above.
To become the salvation of fallen man.

He lifts us up in His Mercy and Grace.
And gives us His spirit of light.
He covers us with His righteousness.
And gives us the gift of sight.

Taking the risk of following "The Shepherd"…
To the Kingdom that has no end.
Finding the Immaculate Love of our Father.
To be our true and faithful Friend.

RAINBOW:
"Come follow me," Jesus said, "and I will make you fishers of men."
Matthew 5:19

TAPESTRY OF LOVE

God wove together in the seed of His Son.
Grace and Truth—life's battle was won.
Son of darkness—Son of Great Light.
Heaven to earth—recovering of sight.

The Son of God—the Son of Man.
Bringing redemption into God's plan.
Joining our spirit in the Son's blood.
Covering the earth with God's Infinite Love.

Weaving our flesh of lust and pride…
Into the bridegroom's soul, for the love of His bride.
Joining together both blood and seed.
Purifying, cleansing, and meeting our need.

Tapestry of Love—uniting of souls.
Cleansing, purifying and making life whole.
Joining together heart, soul, and mind.
Trusting the heart of God's Love Divine.

Kneading Trinity's Love without leaven
Into earth's seed—the pure bread of Heaven.
He walked among scavengers, death, and destruction.
Was nailed to the cross with this inscription.

"Jesus of Nazareth King of the Jews."
Mocked, ridiculed, denied, and scourged.
Crowned with thorns, spit on, and betrayed.
In an open sepulcher His body was laid.

Blood spilled on the earth—flesh buried in the ground.
Redemption was complete—the doctrine was sound.
Arose on the third day—returned to "The Creator."
King of the Universe—intercessor and mediator.

Pure, sincere, just, faithful, and true.
God's unconquerable Love for me and for you.
A crown of thorns for a crown of glory.
Nothing compares to God's love story.

RAINBOW:
I delight greatly in the Lord; my soul rejoices in my God. For He has clothed me with garments of salvation and arrayed me in a robe of righteousness, as a bridegroom adorns his head like a priest, and as a bride adorns herself with her jewels. For as the soil makes the sprout come up and a garden causes seed to grow, so the sovereign Lord will make righteousness and praise spring up before all nations.
Isaiah 61:10-11

THAT IS WHY

Satan doesn't have any power.
Satan doesn't have any love.
Satan doesn't have any righteousness.
It comes from our Father above.
That is why I keep praising.
That is why I keep singing.
That is why Love is amazing.
That is why the church bells are ringing.

Satan doesn't have any truth.
Satan doesn't have any grace.
Santa doesn't have any mercy.
He has no resting place.
That is why I keep searching.
That is why I keep knocking.
That is why I keep reaching.
That is why I keep asking.

Satan doesn't have any hope.
Satan doesn't have any joy.
Satan doesn't have any peace.
He is a thief, a counterfeit, a decoy.
That is why I keep believing.
That is why I keep hoping.
That is why I keep receiving.
That is why I keep coping.

Satan doesn't give any life.
Satan doesn't have any resurrection.
He causes division, confusion, and strife.
That is why I keep reading.
That is why I keep praying.
That is why I keep heeding.
That is why I keep saying.

Satan doesn't have any promises.
Satan doesn't have a redemption plan.
Satan doesn't have any stability.
Security is in God's trusting hand.
That is why I keep clinging to Jesus and His cross.
Cleaving to His Holy name.
Gleaning God's Infinite Word.
That changes not and always the same.

RAINBOW:
A faith and knowledge resting on the hope of eternal life, which God, who does not lie, promised before the beginning of time. And at his appointed season He brought His word to light through the preaching entrusted to me by the command of God our Savior.
Titus 1:2

THE ADVENT

God looked down from the Heavens above…
See His children void of pure love.
He gathered His angels all over the sky…
And he bid His Beloved Son to draw very nigh.

I am sending you as a spotless lamb…
The sacrificial atonement for sin as a ram.
You will be born as a baby in a virgin's womb…
To expose evil's darkness and empty death's tomb.

Death will be broken through the cross of Calvary.
Healing of nations from the life in "The Tree"…
My covenant with Moses, David, and Abraham.
Fashioned the Word made flesh as "The Great I Am."

You will fulfill the Old Testament down through the ages.
Sealing the New Testament's blood with Holy Pages.
Born as a baby in a stable in Bethlehem.
With a name of deity—Jehovah, Adonai, Elohim.

Your footprints on earth will never be erased…
A crown of glory will forever shine on the human race.
You will feel every infirmity and weakness of sin.
A new life in your spirit of My Love will begin.

As the dead of winter gives birth to the spring…
A resurrection of hope to my children you will bring.
Christmas and Easter will be a time of celebration.
Your death will bring forth new life and resurrection.

Your name will be a name above every name…
A sign that My Holy Love will never change.
I will be in you every step of "the Way."
You will gather my sheep who have gone astray.

The promise I made to Abraham you will fulfill…
Earth will be blessed through your cross on Calvary's hill.
Leave with them this promise so faithful and true.
"I will never leave you, nor forsake you."

RAINBOW:
Therefore the Lord Himself shall give you a sign; behold, the virgin shall conceive, and bear a Son, and shall call His name Immanuel.
Isaiah 7:14

THE COVENANT

In this world we live, below.
Brokenness will always be…
There is one thing mindful…
We all need to know.
Brokenness is a way of life…
As far as mortal man can explain.
In the river, ocean, land, and sea.
This is the nature of fallen things.
Broken vows and broken dreams.
We seek, and pray for the Father's will.
This is the nature of fallen things.
Broken hearts, we hurt and cry.
We ask the question—why oh why.
This is the nature of fallen things.
Broken homes that need repair…
We seek for love to rule and reign.
Hopelessly and in despair…
This is the nature of fallen things.

The awe and the wonder of nature's fall…
God is in our brokenness—God is in all.
God sees—God knows—God understands.
He holds the universe in His Holy hands.
This is His body—that was broken for us…
Take—eat—to remember God's Infinite Love.
This cup is His blood—He took our curse.
Drink to remember our unity with God above.
He opened up Heaven's throne room…
Where He sits with God on high.
To intercede in all of our earthly prayers…
With Grace and Truth that will never die.
He heals the brokenhearted.
Sets the captive free…
He preached the gospel to the poor.
Opened blinded eyes to see.
God sees our brokenness…
He joins us—flesh and bone.
Through Jesus' blood and Jesus' name…
He claims us for His own.

RAINBOW:
And when he had given thanks to God for it. He broke it and gave it to His disciples and said, "Take this and eat it. This is my body, which is given for you. Do this to remember Me." In the same way, he took the cup of wine after supper, saying. "This is the new agreement between God and you that has been established and set in motion by my blood. Think of this in remembrance of me whenever you drink it. For ever time you eat this bread and drink this cup you are re-telling the message of the Lord's death; that He had died for you. Do this until He comes again."
1 Cornithians 11: 24-26

THE ABIDING PLACE

Come, all you weary people…
Burdened down with care.
There is an eternal abiding place.
Not filled with doubt or fear.

There is "The Great Shepherd"…
With spotless blood and seed.
Behold! "The Lamb of God."
Who supplies our every need.

He will lead us in green pastures.
The sheep of His fold.
Feed us with His Spirit…
Our dry and barren soul.

He feels all of our infirmities.
He knows our every need.
The Beloved Son of God…
Born of righteous seed.

When we are lonely and sad.
When we suffer with pain and sorrow.
He is "The Faithful One."
Yesterday, today, and tomorrow.

He will take our every burden.
He knows our every care.
He is "The Trusted Friend"…
Even in our despair.

God has given us an invitation…
To bask in Heaven's Son.
The joy of being loved…
By the True and Faithful One.

The forever abiding place…
In His Kingdom, Power, and Glory.
God feeding us His life-giving spirit…
Through His Son's love story.

RAINBOW:
Take care to live in Me, and let Me live in you. For a branch can't produce fruit when severed from the vine. Nor can you be fruitful apart from me.
John 15:4

THE ALL SUFFICIENT ONE

In God so weak…
That He cannot uphold His Word?
Are His hands so short…
That He cannot serve?

Are His ears so heavy…
That He cannot hear?
Is He so far away…
That we have no fear?

God has given us…
His Love through His Son…
To comfort us on earth…
Until our work is done.

All of earth's blessings comes…
From the Heavens above.
The gift of Grace, Truth, and Mercy…
Created by God's Infinite Love.

The pathway to Heaven…
Is though the Lord's blood.
Anointed by His Holy Spirit…
With wisdom, power, and love.

Can there be a better plan…
Than the works of God's hand?
Can there be a better place
Than God's Love, Truth, and Grace?

We, like Job, may suffer loss…
God's redemptive plan included the cross.
When we are crucified with Him…
There is light without darkness and love without sin.

Somewhere deep within our souls…
We must comprehend…
God's Love is not for cowards…
But for extraordinary men!

RAINBOW:
Surely the arm of the Lord is not too short to save, nor His ear too dull to hear. But your iniquities have separated you from your God.
Isaiah 59:1-2

THE BLESSING

God blessing creation was very good…
With freedom of life in Jesus' blood.
Blessing of love, joy, and peace…
Through the Holy Spirit will increase.

Greater is God's Love that lives in me…
Greater is His truth that has set men free…
Greater is His forgiveness, mercy, and grace…
Greater is Jesus, who took sin's place.

God's gift of His blood in the Son's righteous seed…
For earth's redemption to supply our spiritual need.
His righteous seed of joy, peace, and love…
Heals broken hearts with truth from above.

Oh, the burdens we bear of living on earth…
Rejecting God's blessings in the new spiritual birth.
Denying the Word of God's promise so true…
Nor claiming the blessing of each day being new.

In God's blood and righteous seed…
His Living Word meets our every need.
Resurrection to a new life begins at the cross.
Jesus giving spiritual blessing from nature's loss.

Loving God with all our heart, soul, and mind…
Brings blessings from Heaven all the time.
Where God's Truth and Grace abide…
Sin's darkness can never hide.

Washed in the spotless blood of the Lamb.
Joined by the cross to "The Great I Am."
Jesus shares life's blessing from "The Creator."
With Majestic Power, Glory, Honor as "The Mediator."

The blessing we ponder—the blessing we deny…
From our Father's throne room on high.
With doubts and fears—with sadness and tears.
Oh the blessing we reject days, months, and years.

Wisdom cries at the door and continues to knock…
To build life's foundation on the Spiritual Rock.
God's gives blessing—more than we can receive…
As we open our hearts to "The Acts" and believe.

RAINBOW:
In a loud voice they sang: "Worthy is the Lamb, who was slain, to receive power and wealth and wisdom and strength and honor and glory and praise!"
Revelation 5:12

THE BLOOD COVENANT

More precious than silver or gold…
Is "The Spirit" of God to man's soul.

The incorruptible seed sown into the earth.
Was God's gift of love for man's new birth.

After "The Blood" fell to the ground…
Communion with God was Holy and Sound.

"The Blood" paid in full our redemption…
"The Truth" brought freedom for all generations.

Resurrection was cradled in "The Word"…
His Blood and Body is now being served.

God's covenant sealed by "The Blood" is pure…
Rooted, grounded, established, certain, and sure.

In the eye of "The Spirit" is "The Word" of "The Son"…
When He spoke "It is finished" His work was done.

Have faith in "The Light" of "The Word" that is spoken…
Where sin chains of darkness and deception are broken.

God created "The Covenant" for me and for you…
"The Blood" in "The Word" is faithful and true.

Salvation to the earth is Heaven's gift from…
God the Father—God the Spirit—God the Son.

There is a new song in the heart of man to sing…
Jesus is my Lord—my Savior—my King.

RAINBOW:
And now may the God of Peace, who brought again from the dead our Lord Jesus, equip you with all you need for doing His will. May he who became the great Shepherd of the sheep by an everlasting agreement between God and you, signed with His blood, produce in you through the power of Christ all that is pleasing to Him. To Him be the glory forever and ever. Amen.
Hebrews 13:20-21

THE BRIDEGROOM

Someone does care for you…
In the depths of your heart.
He is waiting and wooing…
And searching the dark.
Someone is very close…
And needs you to know…
Inside the door of your heart…
God's seed of faith—He will sow…
To reveal the mystery…
Of love without end
Handed down through history…
Is a record of this constant Friend.
He will never leave, nor forsake you…
Never lead you astray.
Somewhere deep inside…
The reservoir of your soul.
Is the living water of life…
To live in you and make you whole.
There is someone just for you…
You can depend on to take you through…
This world of temptation, deception, and sin.
God prepared a place—where death has no sting.
The pure love of God will forever reign.
It is not very long on this earth below…
Heed His voice and your heart will know.

> Listen and learn this great mystery of life…
> In Jesus' spirit—there is no struggle or strife.
> The lover and bridegroom of earthly souls…
> Will give you more love than your heart can hold.

RAINBOW:
The crowds will naturally go to the main attraction – the bride will go where the bridegroom is ! A bridegroom's friends rejoice with him. I am the bridegroom's friend, and I am filled with joy at His success. He must become greater and greater, and I must become less and less. He has come from heaven and is greater than anyone else. I am of the earth, and my understanding is limited to the things of earth.
John 3:29-31

THE CHRISTMAS STORY

Nowhere can we go that love is not near.
Love is the reason we give and we share.
Love has its roots in our Savior the King.
Love is the reason for the church bells to ring.
Love is endowed by God, the Creator of Heaven and earth.
Love is the reason for our new spiritual birth.
God gave us the gift of His perfect Love…
That reaches from earth to the Heavens above.
Love overcomes darkness, deception, and fear…
Sadness, grief, burden, death, and despair,
Each time we face temptation and sin…
God sees our Savior's blood and His Love wins.
Rooted, grounded, and established in God's Love…
We are one with our Savior who came from above.
Love conquered death, the wages of sin…
Opening death's tomb: to let God's Light come in.
You see whatever we suffer—whatever we face.
Love conquered the fall of the human race.
God has made us a promise so faithful and true.
Love will never mock, condemn, or forsake you.
He brings comfort, wisdom, and strength…
To those who are poor—to those who are weak.
So hold fast to the provision of your faith.
Love has no death—Love has no hate.
It all came together at the foot of "The Cross."
When Love made the provision to pay sin's cost.

Now we are free in God's perfect Love…
From the cradle of birth—to the Heavens above.
Love one another is God's divine plan…
Love is the working of God's Holy hand.
In God's Infinite Love we live and abide.
There is no place on earth where sin can hide.
You see, God made us to be like Him…
Without darkness, deception, and sin.
We are walking by faith in Truth and Grace.
And seated with Him in the heavenly place.
In His Kingdom of Power, Honor, and Glory…
God poured out His Love in the birth of His story.
Love is the rise of nature's fall…
God is love and love conquers all.

RAINBOW
No, in all of these things we are more than conquerors through Him who loved us.
Romans 8:37

THE CLASS OF '55

Let our thoughts go back to yesteryear.
When our days were filled with laughter and tears.
Think of those nostalgic days at Pavo School.
When things were simple and we followed the rules.

We have traveled down life's road since '55…
Erasing all thoughts that we had finally arrived.
Each given a book with empty pages to write.
Creating our own story of each day and night.

Walking amid sunshine and rain…
Mountains, valleys, deserts, and plains.
We learned how to find joy in our sorrow.
Always looking for a better tomorrow.

We have drank our cup of bitterness…
And shared our cup of joy.
We felt the pain of loneliness…
That life on earth does employ.

We've had our share of problems to solve…
Some we thought could never be resolved.
We have walked in the footprints of God and man on earth…
Struggled with the two Adams who gave us this birth.

Fought endless battles of loss and gain…
Death, darkness, sorrow suffering, and pain.
Love, joy, peace, laughter, smiles, and tears…
A loom of life's pattern down through the years.

We took separate paths down life's road…
A tapestry of life's seeds we have sowed.
All woven together in the master plan…
The battle of life—the works of God's hand.

RAINBOW:
His winnowing fork is in His hand to clear His threshing floor and to gather wheat into His barn, but he will burn up the chaff with unquenchable fire."
Luke 3:17

Dedicated to the Class of '55 - Pavo High School, Pavo, GA

THE COMING JOY

God created new life in His Son's love story…
Revealing His Truth, His Grace, and His Glory.
Our body is the temple of the loving Word.
The sweetest love song—one's soul has ever heard.

We live, and breathe, and have our being in Him…
Where love never fades and the light never dims.
Faith, Hope, and Love is the Biblical cord…
In the Kingdom of God where Jesus is Lord.

Heaven was listening to the Words of God's Son…
When He cried, "Not my will on earth, but your will be done."
The angels were waiting at Heaven's door…
To welcome the King of kings and the Lord of lords.

His visitation is remembered as "Our Lord's Day on Earth."
When God redeemed humanity and gave us a new birth.
Christ in us—the hope of His glory…
These pages are written in "The Greatest Love Story."

When the people of earth receive God's message of love…
They are redeemed by the gift of the Savior's blood.
He is patiently calling His earthly children one by one…
To abide in "The Father, The Spirit, The Son."

We are safe in His Grace and Truth forevermore…
Faith is "The Key" that opens "The Door."
Never more to wonder—never more to fear…
God comforts our sorrows and wipes away each tear.

Joy, peace, and love is the gift for our sorrow and pain…
Our loss on this earth is Heaven's great gain.
Wait patiently, My children—wait for the dawning…
Weeping may endure for the night—but joy comes in the morning.

RAINBOW:
Sing to the Lord, you saints of his: praise His Holy name. For His anger last only a moment, but His favor lasts a lifetime, weeping may remain for a night, but rejoicing comes in the morning.
Psalms 30:5

THE CRY OF THE SOUL

Open our souls to the window of God.
Shepherd us as sheep with Your staff and Your rod.
Let us live in earth's nature as God's little lamb.
To be comforted and strengthened by "The Great I Am."

Let our mind be in Christ—Our heart rest in God.
Holy Spirit to guide our feet in the footprints of love.
Our hands to serve in righteousness and peace.
Faith in "The One" that causes the storms to cease.

Ears for listening to the sound of God's voice.
In the presence of "The Holy One"—our hearts rejoice.
Our countenance to shine with Jesus' glory.
Our tongue, telling His great love story.

Daily remind us of "The Gift" of Your Love.
The cross that united earth to the Heavens above.
Your invitation to come, taste, and see…
The truth in Jesus—that sets our spirit free.

Guiding us through this world of temptation and sin.
To love and be loved by our Shepherd and Friend.
Let us strive to be like Him in all of our ways.
Our souls singing, exalting, and giving God praise.

Let the earth rejoice—the Heavens sing.
The angels come forth—the church bells ring.
Peace on earth—good will toward men.
Celebrating "The Baby" born in Bethlehem.

RAINBOW:
For You O Lord, have delivered my soul from death, my eyes from tears, my feet from stumbling that I may walk before the Lord in the land of the living.
Psalms 116:8

THE DIVINE SHEPHERD

Unto the Heavens we will focus…
To our home beyond the sky.
Sitting at God's right hand is
The Shepherd's Love we must not deny.

He is making intercession for us…
As we live below the sky.
He is watching over us.
With His all-seeing eye.

We must continue in our praying…
In prayers that will never cease.
For our prayers availeth much…
For His lambs and His lost sheep.

He tells us not to wander…
Far away from His fold and tender care.
For wolves will devour His little lambs.
We must never cease in prayer.

We are like sheep, ready for the slaughter…
Who needs God's protection and care.
The wolves are out to devour us.
Let us come to God in prayer.

Jesus said, "I am the great Shepherd...
I will lead you in pastures that are green.
By the streams of living waters.
Protect you as a chick underneath My wing."

Cleave and stay close to "The Shepherd."
Learn to hear His voice when we pray.
He will lead us away from temptation...
Keep us from the evil of the day.

He is "The Good Shepherd."
His sheep learn to hear His voice.
When we follow His leading...
Our hearts are made to rejoice.

He prepares a table before us.
Right in the presence of our foe.
With Truth and Grace to sustain us.
His goodness and mercy we shall know.

RAINBOW:
My sheep recognize my voice, and I know them, and they follow me. I give them eternal life and they shall never perish. No one shall snatch them away from me.
John 10:27-28

THE GIFT OF A FRIEND

God has given me a gift in you.
Whether I am happy, sad, or blue.
Someone to listen and not condemn
Someone to share when life seems dim.

Someone to bring sunshine out of a cloud.
Calming the spirit when things seem turbulent and loud.
Someone who loves God and shares the good news.
No matter what happens we can never lose.

Someone to listen—someone to care.
Someone to love—someone to share.
In earth's joy and sorrow.
Someone to encourage a brighter tomorrow.

Creating a way to make life worth living…
Sharing our hearts with a friend is a true art of giving.
While we live on earth amid darkness and sin.
God's gift is a gift of a wonderful friend.

RAINBOW:
A friend loves at all times, and a brother is born for adversity.
Proverbs 17:17

In memory of Dotty Tucker, who was a true friend.

THE GIFT OF CHOICE

Jesus is "The Gift" we give ourselves.
The gift of Eternal Love.
Full of God's blessings…
Coming down from the Heavens above.

Love—is in the gift…
From Life's inherited tree.
Our resurrection from the grave.
A gift of eternity.

Grace and Truth—is in the Gift…
No charge—no fee.
Purchased by the Lamb's pure blood…
On the cross of Calvary.

Trust—is in the gift…
Built on Love's foundation.
Not life, nor death, can take it away…
The beginning of all creation.

Forgiveness—is in the gift…
The song of our salvation.
All in the name of Jesus…
God's gift of reconciliation.

Hope—is in the gift…
Entwined with faith and love.
A threefold cord cannot be broken…
United with the Savior's spotless blood.

Peace—is in the gift…
From the pages of God's Word.
The greatest voice of victory…
One's soul has ever heard.

Faith—is in the gift…
Straight from our Father's heart.
Without faith it is impossible…
For God's Love to impart.

Life—is in the Gift…
Sown by the seed of the righteous One…
While living upon nature's earth.
God's miracle of a spiritual birth.

RAINBOW:
But whatever is good and perfect comes to us from God, the creator of all light, and he shines forever without change or shadow.
James 1: 17

THE GREATEST IS LOVE

Love is God...
Love is Supreme.
Love is the Master...
Over everything.

Love is the Conqueror...
Of darkness, death, and sin.
Love is the Light...
Where Deity shines in.

Love is God's Word...
Love is time.
Love is true, and patient...
Faithful, long-suffering, and kind.

Love is Truth and Grace...
Love is joy and peace.
Love is humility and meekness
Love will never cease.

Love and live...
Is the Master's call.
Redeemed by the blood.
Love conquers all.

In sorrow, in grief, in pain…
In storms, in clouds, in rain.
In the cross and in the crown.
Love is complete and renown.

Love is redemption…
Love paid sin's cost.
Love laid God's heart …
At the foot of the cross.

RAINBOW:
In the same way, we can see and understand only a little about God now, as if we were peering at His reflection in a poor mirror; but someday we are going to see Him in His completeness face to face. Now all that I know is hazy and blurred, but then I will see everything clearly, just as clearly as God sees into my heart right now. There are three things that remain. Faith—Hope—Love and the greatest of these is love.
1 Corinthians 13:13

THE IMMACULATE HEART

The heart of our Heavenly Father…
In Whom there is no other.
So immaculate, pure, and true.
Our sin in the heart—He could not view.

God's Love was so great—He became man…
So the law of the universe could expand.
From Heaven to earth through the cross of His Son…
In the heart of God's Love—life's battle was won.

He became flesh to set our spirit free…
When He laid down His life for you and for me.
Jesus sowed the seed of God's righteousness…
To give earth—Heaven's blessedness.

In His Son's Spirit was God's new creation.
Illuminating His Love—a light for all nations.
The Kingdom of God's Love that was rooted in Heaven.
Giving birth to the earth—bread without leaven.

The pure Love of the Son's sacred heart…
Fulfilled Moses' law—the covenant of the ark.
Fire and water for purification.
The righteous seed for sanctification.

God gave birth when His soul travailed…
Through faith, we honor His word and His will.
There is no other name in the universe…
That can break nature's sin—our inherited curse.

RAINBOW:
But in your hearts set apart Christ as Lord… Always be prepared to give an answer to everyone who asks you to give the reason for the hope that you have. But do this with gentleness and respect.
1 Peter 3:15

THE KINGDOM WITHIN

There is a beautiful kingdom within the soul.
An immaculate kingdom complete and made whole.
Where God lives and no sins abound.
Jesus' Glory is all around.

No death, deception, or darkness will intrude.
Love is supreme and love rules.
We are all one in His incorruptible seed.
God lives in us and supplies our need.

Where life is eternal—God's Word never ends.
Jesus' blood covers all of our sin.
There is peace and joy—His Spirit gives light.
His Love illuminates the darkest of nights.

Search the Scriptures and you will find.
God is never late—He is right on time.
He gives the Kingdom to all that believe.
God's Spirit is Truth—our flesh deceives.

Heaven's blessings came from nature's curse.
God's Word governs the universe.
Look deep within your heart, soul, and mind.
His life has been there all the time.

Look to Jesus and you will see.
His Spirit gives grace and liberty.
There is no place for sin to hide.
When Jesus is Lord and truth abides.

Jesus in us—we were crucified in Him.
Nailed to His cross was our nature called sin.
We are seated with Him in the heavenly place.
Sealed by His Spirit—His Truth—His Grace.

See, God's children, how special you are!!!
Love lay in the manager and Love was the Star.
Love hung on the cross with all of our sin.
God is love and love never ends.

RAINBOW:
For He has rescued us out of the darkness and gloom of Satan's kingdom and brought us into the Kingdom of His dear Son, who bought our freedom with His blood and forgave us all our sins.
Colossians 1:13-14

THE LIGHT OF MEN

The Will of God is the work of His hand…
God's Word was His passion and command

His voice speaks words of Truth and Grace…
His Spirit is man's abiding place.

His thoughts and ways are faithful and true.
His mind and heart brought forth the new.

His righteous seed sown in the earth.
Gave light to men in their spiritual birth.

His countenance shines with God's Glory…
The way of life is in His story.

Straight and narrow is His way.
His Spirit is our strength each day.

He is the master of life and man's security.
His walk was the walk of grace and purity.

Living and breathing and having His being in God
Gives God's children Eternal Love.

RAINBOW:
In Him was life; and the life was the light of men.
John 1:4

THE LION AND THE LAMB

Coming together in the—new spiritual birth…
The culmination of Heaven and earth.
The Lion of Judah–the Lamb of God.
One creation of Eternal Love.

The time we spend on earth in sorrow and sadness…
Will come together in joy and gladness.
The lion and the lamb will lie down as one…
In the green pasture of—"The Righteous Son."

In Heaven and earth's culmination…
Eternity to spend in celebration.
Father Time and Mother Earth.
Will glory forever through our Savior's birth.

The highest pinnacle of God's creative Love…
The Lion of Judah and the Lamb of God.
No sin—nor sickness will darken the day.
No death, nor sorrow in the Son's glorious ray.

The Lamb and the Lion will lie down as one.
In completion to the story of God and His Son.
The beginning of no end.
Rejoicing together with our greatest friend.

One in the spirit of Truth and Grace.
One with the Savior who took sin's place.
One in Jesus' body, heart and mind.
One with "The Master" all the time.

One in the redeemer's righteous seed…
One in "The One" who supplies our every need.
The Creator culminating "The Greatest Love Story."
To God in the highest: Glory! Glory! Glory!

RAINBOW:
Then one of the elders said to me. "Do not weep! See, the Lion of the tribe of Judah, the root of David, has triumphed. He is able to open the scroll and its seven seals."
Revelation 5:5

THE MARRED IMAGE

Looking in the mirror of God's Law…
Seeing God's Love without a flaw.
Viewing holiness as perfection…
Grace and Truth in earth's correction.

Nature falls short of God's Infinite Glory…
His image mirrors the Son's life story.
Seeing the reflection of God in the Son.
His Kingdom established—finished—well done.

The cross embraces the scars He bore…
Nature reveals the crown of thorns He wore.
Redeeming Love—the song of the universe.
Imagining God's blessing greater than Adam's curse.

Jesus is the Light—we are the window…
Hold fast the light for joy and for splendor.
The "Son of Righteousness" reflects the earth.
Giving human nature—Heaven's birth.

Hear the sound of nature's voice…
Rejoice! Rejoice! Rejoice!
Christ is risen indeed!
Through His Spirit—God leads.

Truth and righteousness—the purity of bread…
Through God's Spirit—His children are fed.
Don't be discouraged in nature's fall.
The Lord of Love—reigns above all.

Look in the mirror—see your reflection in Him…
Practice and practice and practice again.
See yourself as God's special child.
Hold fast His image and smile, smile, smile.

RAINBOW:
Now we see but a poor reflection as in a mirror; than we shall see face to face. Now I know in part; than I shall know full, even as I am full known. And now these three remain; faith, hope, and love But the greatest of these is love.
1 Corinthians 13:12-13

THE MASTER

Jesus is "The Master" of both old and new.
He is "The One" who is faithful and true.
Giving Him this fleshly life we were born in…
Frees us from deception, darkness, and sin.

We are none holy—neither can we be.
God's gift of Jesus—alone sets us free.
He is the Master of God's Love Divine.
The Master of the earth—The Master of time.

He is the master of the ship on the turbulent sea.
The Master of emotions though troubled they may be.
He is the Master of the wind and the shifting sand,
He is the Son of God—the Son of Man.

He is the Master of Truth—the Master of Grace.
The Master of Spirit—the soul's resting place.
God has put us all in the Master's hand.
We can rest secure in His redemption plan.

Some call Him—Lord—some call Him—King.
Some call Him—The Body—where the church bells ring.
Some call Him—Jehovah—Adonai—Elohim.
The Prince of Peace—The Baby born in Bethlehem.

Some call Him—The Redeemer—The Friend.
Some call Him—The Savior—that takes away sin.
The First Fruits—Alpha—Omega.
The Way—The Truth—The life—The Messiah.

The Vine—The Door—The Shepherd—The Resurrection.
The Bread—The living Water—The Tree.
The Lilly of the Valley—The Teacher—The Most High.
The Holy Spirit—The City on the Hill—The All-Seeing Eye.

The Conqueror—The Sabbath—-The Bright and Morning Star.
All-Sufficient One—The One from Afar.
The Unseen Hand—The Bridegroom—Abba Father—God—The Lamb.
Omnipotence—Omnipresence—Omniscient—The Great I Am.

The Rose of Sharon—The Comforter—The Unseen Hand.
The Light of the World—The Son of God—The Son of Man.
Emanuel—God with Us.
The name above all names…
JESUS

RAINBOW:
You will be with child and give birth to a son, and you are to give Him the name JESUS. He will be great and will be called the Son of the Most High. Luke 1:31-32

THE MASTER ARTIST

After the summer…
Before the winter's low.
When the trees stand naked and barren…
In the cold, rain, ice, and snow.

God mixes colors of fiery red…
Orange, brown, green and yellow.
The Master Artist paints the leaves…
In ravish—dazzle color.

He shines the harvest moon…
And sets the sun aflame.
To the awe and wonder of…
His Majestic Name.

Life begins again…
In the spring.
As he covers the trees…
In a garment of green.

The seasons come…
The seasons go.
Keeping life full of color…
The heart aglow.

Green hills…
Brown desert sands…
Blue oceans that…
Separate the land.

The sun, moon, galaxies of stars.
The sky above…
Give to us the glory of…
God's Eternal Love.

Colors in the rainbow…
God's covenant to show.
The arrow in His hands.
Love is in His bow.

RAINBOW:
For by Him all things were created: things in heaven and on earth, visible and invisible, whether thrones or powers or rulers or authorities; all things were created by Him and for Him. He is before all things, and in Him all things hold together.
Colossians 1:16-17

THE MIND OF GOD

Who can know the mind of God?
Only "The Son," whose feet have trod…
The seed of His thoughts and ways…
Jesus, the Rock of our refuge and stay.

By His roots man's redemption stems…
A rose from a thorn ordering the steps of men.
God gave us His Grace and His Truth…
His Living Word—is living proof.

God made man in His very own image…
He gave us His Word and all that is in it.
Man rejected His Word and the fall began…
Chaos and confusion was the result of man.

To this very day—a division stands…
From the One who holds the universe in His hands.
God has given us an invitation through His Son…
To join in His Spirit and be loved by "The Holy One."

When we reject His Son—we have rejected His call…
To be redeemed from the earth and nature's fall.
Oh the blessing we miss in our earthly division…
When God made His Son—the earth's provision.

As long as we live on earth—we still have His time...
To eat from His incorruptible flesh and drink His pure wine.
Come unto Me is the call of our Heavenly Father...
I have made My Son—LIFE—there is no other.

There is no other way we can claim Heaven's blessings...
From Jesus our Savior—we learn life's great lesson.
The day of redemption and the cross stands...
Joining us to Him through "The God Man."

RAINBOW:
Let this mind be in you, which was also in Christ Jesus, Who, being in the form of God thought it not robbery to be equal with God, But made himself of no reputation, and took upon Him the form of a servant, and was made in the likeness of men.
Philippians 2: 5-8

THE PEARL OF GREAT PRICE

Finding it all in Jesus…
Our Lord, Savior, Redeemer, and King.
Finding the Pearl of Great Price…
In the message that God does bring.

I found the hidden manna of Heaven…
In the sounds of silence I heard…
The sights and wonders of all creation…
When I tasted His Living Word.

I drank from His fountain of living water…
And it quenched the thirst of my soul.
In the spirit of my Savior…
My life was complete and made whole.

My soul longs for your presence…
Every second of the day.
Keep me close to you, O Holy Spirit…
Never let me go astray.

I found "The Pearl of Great Price"…
In the life of God's beloved Son…
I pray every day not my will…
But the will of my Father be done.

Master of all things great and small…
Teach me how to love without sin.
In my thoughts, words, and deeds…
Never let me criticize, judge, or condemn

I found "The Pearl of Great Price."
The Kingdom of Power and Glory.
I have gleaned and tasted the hidden manna…
From the pages of His infinite life story.

RAINBOW:
Again, the kingdom of heaven is like a merchant man, seeking fine pearls, who when he had found one pearl of great price, went and sold all that he had, and bought it.
Matthew 13:45-46

THE PRIZE IN THE HIGH CALLING

Written down and told through the ages…
Is a crown of glory from God's Holy Pages.
The crown of life is hidden in "The Word."
Eyes have not seen—ears have not heard.

We are running a race in this world below…
Through seeds of faith on earth we sow.
The race is to obtain the prize of the crown.
Jesus, "The Author," the name of renown.

What is God's crown? It is His Glory.
Woven into the life of Jesus' love story.
Sin's death was conquered—life's battle was won.
In the name of—The Father—The Spirit—The Son.

Love is the glory—that life does pursue.
God's blessings to earth, so pure, and so true.
He made us a little lower than the angels above.
Redeemed us to wear His crown of pure love.

God's Son was the Firstborn of Glory's Light.
To illuminate the darkness of sin's plight.
Jesus' death gave us salvation's story.
His Spirit—His Crown—His Glory.

RAINBOW:
Let us fix our eyes on Jesus, the author and perfecter of our faith, who for the joy set before Him endured the cross, scorning its shame, and sat down at the right hand of the throne of God.
Hebrews 12:2

THE PROMISE

God's promise was fulfilled in the birth of God's Son.
Death to death—life's battle was won...
The deceiver of life in this world below...
Was put to naught from the deceptive seed he sows.

God gave "The Promise" in the words Jesus spoke.
Breaking life's bondage and death's yoke.
Seek you that are weary and burdened with care...
There is rest, love, and life—the Son wants to share.

There is a new song to sing from the story of old...
Eternal Love has been written and unfolds.
The love story handed down through the ages...
Peace, joy, truth, and light flows from its pages.

The promise of life is in the Savior's hand...
No weapon formed against you is able to stand.
I Am—is willing—I Am—is able...
To feed you God's Spirit from Heaven's table.

The promise was made from "The Word" spoken...
Never to be destroyed—never to be broken.
Written and sealed by the Son's blood...
Eternal life—Eternal Love.

God made all things new in the day of redemption…
Old things passed away—a new creation.
Not in the flesh—but in "The Spirit" of the Son.
God was glorified when His work was done.

RAINBOW:
When He had received the drink, Jesus said, "It is finished," with that, He bowed His head and gave up His Spirit.
John 19:30

THE PROMISE AND THE GIFT

The promise and the gift in the Son's Holy Name.
His Word changes not and is always the same.
The promise and the gift of God's Love Divine.
Eternity is waiting for the end of time.

The bride is waiting for the return of the bridegroom.
He is preparing a mansion with plenty of rooms.
All because God loves us so…
Read His Word often, so you can know.

All the cares and worries of this life are in vain.
All suffering, trials, tribulation, grief, and pain.
Count all flesh as loss and worthless, you see…
Compared to His cross that has set our souls free.

We are all one in this vast universe.
Feeling the pain of sin and its curse.
Love one another was our Savior's command.
You are engraved in the palms of God's Holy hands.

God has given us His spirit as a gift for our soul.
In treasures more precious than silver or gold.
His Kingdom has come and His Will is done…
In the life that we live in the gift of His Son.

He has given us love—as the early morning dew.
He has given us truth—and all things are new.
He has given us healing in His Spirit Divine.
He has given us peace in the gift of time.

He has given us grace in our time of need.
He has given us the gift of His righteous seed.
He has given us forgiveness for all of our sins.
We are more than conquerors as we live in Him.

In Him, we live, breathe, and have our being.
In Him is the gift of spiritual seeing.
In Him, the darkest night is turned to day.
He is our Refuge, our Rock, our Stay.

No one can love us so faithful and true.
No one but God can make all things new.
Our broken hearts—He came to heal.
By His Spirit—our spirit is sealed.

The Heavens and earth will pass away.
The promise in the gift of God's Word will stay.
God in His infinite wisdom of all creation…
Began life anew in His resurrection.

Be still and know that God is God.
In the feet of His righteousness "The Seed" was trod.
He has loved us with an everlasting love.
The promise in the gift comes from above.

God has promised us while we live on earth.
In "The Son" we are sealed in a new spiritual birth.
Nothing can pluck us out of His hand.
The Redeemer is the Savior of fallen man.

RAINBOW:
My Father who has given them to me, is greater than all, no one can snatch them out of my Father's hand. I and the father are one.
John 10:29-30

But what ever is good and perfect comes to us from God, the Creator of all light, and he shines forever without change or shadow. And it was a happy day for Him when He gave us our new lives through the truth of Hs Word, and we became, as it were, the first children in His new family.
James 1:17-18

THE ROAD TO THE UNKNOWN

As I travel the road to the unknown…
Laden with sorrows, heartaches, and tears.
A desolate, foreboding feeling I am all alone…
Facing the enemies of doubts, worries, and fears.

The known is behind me…
Diminishing space, and time.
The unknown is before me…
Taunting my heart, my soul, my mind.

Who can deliver me from my fear and pain…
Who can give me a sound mind…
Who can keep me moral and sane…
While eternity is subduing time.

Only the truth spoke by our Redeemer…
The Conqueror of doubts and fears.
The One who answers our questions…
Through generations of days and years.

Jesus—The Great I Am…
He supplies earth's every need.
He is one with God and man…
He is "The Righteous Seed."

He is our Redeemer, Savior, Salvation's Song…
The lover of our soul, our heart, our mind.
There is joy unspeakable all day long…
While eternity is vanquishing time.

Jesus is the Way to Life…
The soul's Redeemer, Lover, and Friend.
We are leaving behind all struggle and strife…
Christ in us—no death, deception, or sin.

RAINBOW:
No for the Scriptures tell us that for His sake we must be ready to face death at every moment of the day—we are like sheep awaiting slaughter; but despite all this overwhelming victory is ours through Christ who loved us enough to die for us. For I am convinced that nothing can ever separate us from His love. Death can't, life can't. The angels won't, our worries about tomorrow, or where we are high above the sky, or in the deepest ocean – nothing will ever be able to separate us from the love of God demonstrated by our Lord Jesus Christ when He died for us.
Romans 8:36-39

THE SOUL

God in His Mercy, Love, and Creation…
Made Himself of no reputation.

He created a life-giving Spirit in a virgin's womb…
To open the grave to death's tomb.

His Love was so great—He became man…
So the law of the universe could expand.

In His soul was God's new creation…
Giving salt and light to all the nations.

Upon His Word—God established His Love…
Giving us His Spirit from the Heavens above.

A life-giving spirit—when Jesus travailed…
God's Spirit—God's Word—God's Will.

Jesus became flesh—to set our spirit free…
By laying down His life—for you and for me.

When His life's blood fell to the ground…
The earth was blessed—His doctrine was sound.

Faith—Hope—Love—came up to bloom…
On the day Jesus arose and opened death's tomb.

From earth to Heaven through the cross of His Son…
Triumphal love—life's battle was won.

RAINBOW:

It is sown a natural body, it is raised a spiritual body. If there is a natural body, there is also a spiritual body. So it is written: "The first man Adam became a living being"; the last Adam, a life-giving Spirit. The spiritual did not come first, but the natural and after that the spiritual.
1 Corinthians 15:44-46

THE TREE

Awake, O my soul…
Hasten to the tree.
Where Life's mystery is hidden…
And joy awaits thee.

O sad and lonely soul…
Why are you cast down?
Awaken to the sounds of nature…
There is glory all around.

The tree of life…
Feeds the living.
Taste, O my soul…
The tree of life is giving.

In the leaves, the fruit, the root of the tree…
There is healing for all nations…
Bless the Lord, O my soul…
At the wonders in God's creation.

The dead tree that made the cross…
Gives faith, hope and love…
Every good and perfect gift…
Comes from Heaven above.

> Rejoice, O my soul…
> Hear the church bells ring…
> The grave has no victory.
> Death has no sting.

RAINBOW:
He is like a tree planted along a riverbank, with its roots reaching deep into the water – a tree not bothered by the heat nor worried by long months of drought. Its leaves stay green and it goes right on producing all its luscious fruit.
Jeremiah 17:8

THE TRUTH

God has given us His Spirit…
In the gift of His Beloved Son.
The true and faithful Spirit.
Where Truth still marches on.

In this earth—man looks above…
For our flesh has been deceived.
The Love of God is in "The Savior."
In His blood and righteous seed.

In God's Son there is the Word.
In the Word there is God's Truth.
In His Truth His Will is done.
The Living Word is living proof.

What He began in the story…
God completed on the cross.
His Truth, Grace, and Glory
Are still seeking for the loss.

In the New Spiritual Birth.
Was God's redemptive plan.
To cleanse the natural earth.
Redeeming fallen man.

Through the Righteous Seed.
In Jesus' Atoning Blood.
He supplies man's every need.
By offering us...
GOD'S ETERNAL LOVE.

RAINBOW:
To the Jews who had believed Him, Jesus said, "If you hold to my teaching, you are really my disciples. Then you will know the truth, and the truth will set you free."
John 8:31-32

THE VALLEY OF LOSS

There is a deep dark valley within my soul…
Where God's light will always shine.
A place where I count everything lost…
And God's perfect Will is mine.

A place called surrender.
A place where we are set free.
A place in the soul's valley.
God has appointed for you and for me.

A place we give up our struggle.
A place we give up our fight.
A place in God's Truth and Grace.
Where God turns darkness to light.

A place of faith and love.
A place to transform to God's perfect plan.
A place of oneness with "The Master."
Where we place all in His nail-scarred hand.

No more struggle for wealth.
No more struggle for control.
No more struggle in the flesh.
God's Will be done in the heart, mind, and soul.

There is a deep, dark valley in one's heart…
Where God's Love is made supreme.
We count all things on earth as loss.
And Jesus becomes Lord over all things.

A place of growth and maturity…
In the blessings of God's peace and rest.
Where God in His infinite wisdom.
Always knows what is best.

RAINBOW:
What is more, I consider everything a loss compared to the surpassing greatness of knowing Christ Jesus my Lord, for whose sake I have lost all things. I consider them rubbish, that I may gain Christ and be found in him, not having a righteousness of my own that comes from the law, but that which is through faith in Christ. The righteousness that comes from God and is by faith.
Philippians 3:8-9

THE VEIL

The veil between reality and truth…
Was created by man…
Vast deception…
Descending "The Great I Am."

Causing spiritual blindness…
Separating God's Love below…
Incurring earth's darkness…
From the fleshly seeds we sow.

The inherited genes of flesh…
Filthy rags of reality…
The corruptible seeds…
Joins God's truth of immortality.

What is in the flesh…
That God would join…
The seed of His Holy Spirit…
In the gift of His Son?

Consummating flesh with spirit…
With His own blood and seed…
In Holy Union…
For all eternity.

His word of honor…
His truth to proclaim…
To a world that sits in darkness…
There is light in Jesus' Name.

RAINBOW:
Therefore, brothers, since we have confidence to enter the Most Holy Place by the blood of Jesus, by a new and living way opened for us through the veil, that is His body, and since we have a great priest over the house of God, let us draw near to God with a sincere heart in full assurance of faith, having our hearts sprinkled to cleanse us from a guilty conscience and having your bodies washed with pure water. Let us hold unswervingly to the hope we profess, for He who promised is faithful.
Hebrews 10:16-23

THE WEAVER

The sorrow of earth—the joy of Heaven.
Is in the Master Weaver's hand.

In all of His Love He weaves them together…
To make us salt and light of the land.

Without sorrow—there could be no joy.
Without darkness—light could not comprehend.

Without spirit—there would be no life.
Without struggles—there would be no strife.

Without flesh—there would be no death.
Without death—there would be no resurrection.

Without the weak—there would be no strong.
Without the right—there would be no wrong.

Without labor—there would be no pain.
Without loss—there would be no gain.

It took the work of the Weaver's hand…
To create the Divine Master Plan.

He finished the loom in the story of His Son.
Giving us His life and making us one.

In all of His Love He weaves us together…
Underneath His wings—underneath His shelter.

Flesh and spirit—darkness and light.
Sun of the earth—stars of the night.

Joy of Heaven—sorrow of earth.
The loom was completed in the Savior's birth.

RAINBOW:
For He has rescued us out of the darkness and gloom of Satan's kingdom and brought us into the Kingdom of his dear Son, who bought our freedom with His blood and forgave us all our sins.
Colossians 1:13-14

THE WONDER OF WONDERS

With all of God's creation so vast and so small.
Why would He bother with humanity at all?
Why did He give us a longing for life and love?
If He had not created a plan from the Heavens above.

Why do we struggle with all of our might…
With our flesh of humanity with fear and a fight?
Does God need us as much as we need Him?
Is His Spirit the gift where the light never dims?

Why was death and redemption a part of His plan…
In His promise to redeem the soul of man?
Why does He humble us and draw us to Him…
Does the blood of the Lamb take away sin?

Sometimes I wonder in doubts and in fears…
How God plans to wipe away all of our tears.
Is the groaning of our old nature worth all the sighs?
Did Jesus exalt us with Him to His throne room on high?

Did God make His Love to humanity known?
By His divine blood were our sins atoned?
Who else could love us so pure and so true…
Or give us a gift that would make all things new?

Just in case you ever wondered like me…
Jesus gave the invitation to come, taste, and see.
All of our earthly flesh is counted as loss.
God gave us His Kingdom by the way of the cross.

RAINBOW:
And He closed the book, and He gave it again to the minister, and sat down. And the eyes of all of them that were in the synagogue were fastened on Him. And he began to say unto then, this day is this scripture fulfilled in your ears. And all bore Him witness and wondered at the gracious words which proceeded out of his mouth. And they said, is not this Joseph's son?
Luke 4:20-22

THROUGH THE EYES OF FAITH

In all of my joys and sorrows.
In all of my todays and tomorrows.
In all my grief and pain.
I see God in everything.

In my laughter and in my tears.
In my sadness and in my fears.
In my losses and in my gains.
I see God in everything.

In my darkness and in my light.
In my days and in my nights.
In the drought and in the rain.
I see God in everything.

In the fire and in the cold.
In the earth and in my soul.
In the fall and in the spring.
I see God in everything.

In my birth and in my life.
In my struggles and in my strife.
In my weakness He does reign.
I see God in everything.

When God became flesh so I could be
In Him and He could be in me.
How wonderful, awesome, and strange.
That I can see God in everything.

In my death and in my resurrection.
In my desire and in my correction.
In my thoughts, heart, and mind.
How marvelous to see God all the time.

I see Him as the Baby and as the Lamb.
I see Him as the Door and The Great I Am
I see him as the Shepherd of the sheep.
I see Him as the Bread and the Wheat.

I see God as the Word and the Creator.
I see Him as the Intercessor and the Mediator.
I see him as the Truth and the Vine.
I see him as the Blood and the Wine.

I see Him as the Sword and the Shield.
I see him as the New Testament and the Will…
I see him as the Rock and the Stay.
I see him as the Light and the Way.

The Father—The Master—The Creator—The Friend.
　Pouring out His soul for the offering of sin.
　I see Him sitting at the Father's right hand.
　Alpha—Omega with no Beginning or End.

　I see him called Jesus—Carpenter—Salvation.
Wonderful—Counselor—mighty God in all creation.
Rose of Sharon—Lily of the Valley—Prince of Peace
　Everlasting Love—that will always increase.

　　I see him as Time—Space—Eternity.
　　Resurrection of Life—a certainty.
I see Him as Lord—Savior—Redeemer—and King.
　　It is no wonder I see God in everything.

RAINBOW:
After Jesus said this, He looked toward heaven and prayed: "Father, the time has come. Glorify your son, that Your son may glorify You. For You granted him authority over all people that he might give eternal life to all those you have given Him. Now this is eternal life: that they may know you, the only true God, and Jesus Christ, whom you have sent. I have brought You glory on earth by completing the work You gave me to do. And now, Father, glorify Me in your presence with glory I had with You before the world began."
John 17:1-5

TIME AND ETERNITY

The shortness of time and the length of eternity…
Gives God's plan for life and love—infinity.
Earth's life is a vapor—the fading of a flower.
In the fullness of time—there is no hour.

Flesh is a gift of all things on earth.
God offered Himself for man's spiritual birth.
Eternity reigns in righteousness and Love of the Son.
When Heaven and earth consummated as one.

No sorrow or tears will ever be known.
No seed of iniquity will ever be sown.
This is the promise of God's Holy Word.
In the voice of the Trinity—God's Truth is heard.

Eye has not seen—heart has never understood.
How God prepared eternity through His pure blood.
Eternity is waiting for you and for me.
Jesus' blood atoned for our sin at Calvary.

Nature groans and sighs and our soul yearns.
While patiently waiting for the Bridegroom's return.
It is not very long that our soul has to wait.
Time joins eternity at Heaven's golden gate.

Place all flesh on God's altar of Love.
A sacrifice of sweet-smelling savor to our Father above.
Prayers of the saints are offered up and sent.
And the angels rejoice when one soul repents.

Search your heart and see if love is not worthwhile.
Turn the other cheek and walk the extra mile.
While we toil and labor sowing the righteous seed.
Love will surely overcome and fill our spiritual need.

Jesus said, "Love one another as I have loved you."
Unconditionally, pure, faithful, and true.
My Love is yours and you are Mine.
Eternity waits where life is not measured by time.

There is a shortness of time while we live on this earth.
Joy is in giving and living the new miracle birth.
Love heals and covers a multitude of sin.
Love one another for love has no end.

RAINBOW:
We know that the whole creation has been groaning as in the pains of childbirth right up to the present time.
Romans 8:22

TRIUMPH IN JESUS

Sheltered from the storms of life…
From the turbulent sea of struggle and strife.
Form the darkness of sin, death, and despair…
Into God's Immaculate Love and tender care.

From the darkness into the light…
From blindness into sight…
From despair into hope…
From words of truth that Jesus spoke.

Through His blood and righteousness…
There is peace, joy, and blessedness.
Only God alone can love us so…
From His Living Word we learn and grow.

All life on earth is in His seed…
Whether a flower or whether a weed.
Through God's Son—our spirit is fed…
Giving us each day our daily bread.

We count our blessings one by one…
Giving God the praise until our work is done.
Though sad and troubled our hearts may be…
We look to the cross—at the living tree.

Through the cross that bore the Son of Man...
Our spirit is led by His unseen hand.
Our eyes are growing dim—but we see from afar...
The setting of the sun from the eastern star.

Culminating words from the gift of God's Son...
When our course is finished—deliverance will come.
Grave, where is your victory? Death, where is your sting?
Triumph in Jesus—from God's heartstring.

RAINBOW:
When the perishable has been clothed with the imperishable, and the mortal with immortality, than the saying that is written will come true: Death has been swallowed up in victory. Where O grave, is your victory? Where O death, is your sting?
1 Corinthians 15:54-56

TRUST

In all of our ways, let us acknowledge Him.
Our Master, Lord, Savior, and Friend.
He will go with us every step of the way.
Our Rock, our Sword, our Shield, our Stay.

All of God's promises hold steadfast and true.
They were written in blood for me and for you.
In the seed of God's Love Jesus sowed…
A tapestry was woven into the earth below.

There will always be in this world we now know…
Sin, darkness, deception, to help us all grow…
Toward the great light of Truth, Love, and Grace.
From earth's suffering—to God's resting place.

Where else can we find so great a salvation?
Only in God, our Father, the creator of all creations.
For the sin of the earth—Grace and Truth abide.
"The Gift" from our Savior who was crucified.

A new inheritance Jesus gave to you and me.
A "Tapestry of Love" began at Calvary…
In the blood of "The One" who was faithful and true.
Jesus fulfilled the law and all things became new.

RAINBOW:
Trust in the Lord with all your heart and lean not on your own understanding;
In all your ways acknowledge Him, and He will make your paths straight.
Proverbs 3:6

UNVEILED MYSTERY

The world is our cross
The cross is our crown.
There is no other place.
Where Love can be found.

Above the thorns—there is the rose.
From the oceans—the rivers flow.
Behind the clouds—the sun is bright.
In darkness—there is light.

In a storm—there is peace.
In the stillness—the winds cease.
In fire—there is purity.
In God's Love—there is security.

In the eye—there is a tear.
In pain—there is fear.
Above the earth—there are the Heavens.
In creation—the days are seven.

In war—there is death and destruction.
In death—there is life and resurrection.
In God's Word—wisdom reigns.
In His Truth—freedom sings.

From God's seed—life does grow.
In life's mystery—God does know.
In a virgin's womb—truth was born.
In His death—the veil was torn.

In Jesus' Love—there is life's story.
In His Holiness—reigns God's glory.
In His truth—the sinner was saved.
In His resurrection—an opened grave.

In God's gift—we can know.
From His Spirit—life does flow.
From His suffering—blessing comes.
Heaven embraced earth through God's Son.

RAINBOW:
He told them, Unto you it is given to know the mystery of the kingdom of God, but unto those who are outside, all these things are done in parables.
Mark 4:11

WE ARE HEALED

In God's New Testament and Will.
By His stripes we are healed…
We are healed.

Redeemed by the blood of the Lamb.
Heaven's gift of "The Great I Am."
We are healed.

Jesus paid our debt of sin.
Through His death—our life begins.
We are healed!

In God's great redemption plan.
The Son of God—became—the Son of Man.
We are healed!

God sent His Word of "Truth and Grace."
His Righteous Seed took sin's place.
We are healed!

Through God's blood and Jesus' name.
God's goodness and mercy overcame.
We are healed!

Stand upon God's Word. "All things are new."
Sealed, established, steadfast, and true.
We are healed!

RAINBOW
But He was pierced for our transgressions, He was crushed for our iniquities; the punishment that bought us peace was upon Him, and by His wounds we are healed.
Isaiah 53:5

YOURS IS THE KINGDOM

You have clothed us in Your righteousness…
Crowned us with Your glory…
Filled us with Your Spirit…
We sang Holy—Holy—Holy.

In the blood of Jesus…
You have washed us white as snow…
You have given us the victory…
And have defeated all our foes.

You have given us the truth…
In the gift of Your Son.
In His death upon the cross…
Your Eternal Kingdom was done.

Though the world be shaken…
In the earth, sea, and land…
God's gift of infinity…
Through eternity will stand.

Jesus—the Rock of Ages…
Has withstood the test of time…
Jesus—the Living Word.
God's Grace and Love Divine.

Your Kingdom of Power, Riches, Wisdom…
Strength, Honor, Blessings and Glory…
Magnifies Your Living Word.
Transforming nature's story.

RAINBOW:
Do not be afraid little flock, for Your father has been pleased to give you the Kingdom.
Luke 12:32

YOU ARE THERE

Wherever I am—You are there.
In darkness—in light—and in my despair.
Nowhere can I hide from Your all-seeing eye.
Through my thoughts—You hear my heart's cry.

I came to You in the darkness of day…
Your light overcame the shadows of gray…
Your truth embraced the terror of night…
No shadows in turning my blindness to sight.

When I am weary, lonely, and sad…
In Your spirit—my heart is made glad.
When I am empty—then I am full.
From You—my strength—my love—I do pull

When I am weak—then I am strong…
Your spirit sustains me all the day long.
The enemy that lies in wait…
Can never enter love's righteous gate.

Your Love was tested and purified seven times.
Creating me Yours—creating You mine.
Day by day my spirit is renewed.
All of my needs are supplied by You.

You are the Bridegroom of my soul…
I am fulfilled—complete—and made whole.
I'll search the Heavens with my spiritual eye.
Waiting for Your return coming through the sky.

RAINBOW:
Lord, you have been our dwelling place throughout all generations. Before the mountains were born or you brought forth the earth and the world, from everlasting to everlasting you are God.
Psalms 90:1-2

YEARNING

My heart yearns for Thee…
O sinless Lamb of Calvary.
Darkness hides not Your face…
You are my soul's Resting Place.

Beneath the sky of things not seen…
You hide me underneath Your silver wings.
You shelter me from life's groans and sighs…
Seeing a glimpse of Heaven through Your eyes.

Whatever happens to me—happens to You…
The love of my soul faithful and true.
United together through the Son's blood…
Endless life—endless love.

All the beauty in life and love…
Is Yours to give from the Heavens above.
Holding this truth in my heart day and night…
Brings me peace, joy, comfort, and light.

When I am afraid, lonely, and sad…
These are the things that make me glad.
I am Yours and You are mine…
Now, forever, and always in endless time.

Your life—Your Love—You gave to me…
Through the blood of Heaven's trinity.
Thanksgiving, praise, worship, and song…
My heart sings to You all the day long.

RAINBOW:
As the deer pants for streams of water, so my soul pants for you O God. My soul thirsts for God, for the living God.
Psalms 41:1-2

WORDS OF LIFE

Words of Jesus I cannot deny.
He gives Love from God—"THE Most High."
Hope in despair.
God's provision and care.
Love to cast out fear.
Comfort in every tear.
Peace in the storms.
Safety in God's arms.
Courage for tomorrow.
Joy in our sorrow.
Resurrection of life.
Hope in our strife.
Strength in our weakness.
Wisdom in our foolishness.
Righteous seed for conception.
Truth in deception.
Contentment in test.
Grace for our rest.
Living Word to abide in.
Forgiveness for sin.
Mercy and loving kindness.
Sight in blindness.
Words of pure gold.
Cleansing of the soul.
Angels, angels, all around.
Righteousness, order, and harmony abound.

Staff for direction.
Rod for correction.
Blessing from the curse.
Emanuel—God with us.
Strength to serve.
Words, words, magnify Jesus "The Word."
Words of Mercy, Grace, Truth, and Love.
Light, peace, joy, hope, faith, comes from above.
So many words we cannot comprehend.
Ears have not heard—Heart cannot understand.
God and Son join man.
In the Great Redemption Plan.
Comforting words Jesus has spoken.
To worlds of hearts that are troubled and broken.

RAINBOW:
This is the message we have heard from Him and declare to you: God is light; in Him there is no darkness at all. If we claim to have fellowship with Him yet walk in the darkness, we lie and do not live by truth.
1 John 5:6

INDEX

A Grain of Sand in the Hourglass	Page 7
Surrender	Page 9
Angels, Rainbows, and Butterflys	Page 11
Beautiful Feet	Page 13
Begin Again	Page 15
Behold the Lamb	Page 17
Bread of Life	Page 19
Change	Page 21
Christian's Peace	Page 23
Come Taste and See	Page 25
Common and Holy Ground	Page 27
Confrontation	Page 29
Conversation with God	Page 31
Crucified with Christ	Page 33
Cry of the Flesh	Page 34
Day Dawning	Page 36
Day Star	Page 38
Divine Love	Page 40
Earth's Greatest Battle	Page 42
Easter	Page 44
Emotions	Page 46
Exaltation of Jesus	Page 48
Faith in God	Page 50
Family Prayer	Page 51
Finding It All	Page 53
Food for Thought	Page 55
Forever Loved	Page 57
From Calvary's Cross	Page 59
Gifts	Page 61
God's Wonderful Way	Page 63
God's Favor	Page 67
God's Best	Page 69
God's Great Nation	Page 71
God's Temple	Page 73
God's Love Endures Forever	Page 75

God Knows and Understands	Page 77
God Owns It All	Page 79
Holy Trinity	Page 81
Hope	Page 83
Hosanna	Page 85
If	Page 87
Illuminated Love	Page 89
Life	Page 91
Mother	Page 93
In Prayer	Page 95
In Pursuit	Page 97
It Is Written	Page 99
Jesus Be Formed in Us	Page 101
Jesus Is Lord	Page 103
Kingdom Workers	Page 105
Know the Enemy	Page 107
Let It Be	Page 109
Letter to God	Page 110
Looking Within	Page 112
Love's Resting Place	Page 114
Love Reigns	Page 116
More Like Jesus	Page 118
My Everything	Page 120
My Father's Child	Page 122
Never Alone	Page 124
New Beginnings	Page 126
Numbered and Named	Page 128
Oh Glorious Dawning	Page 130
Old Things	Page 132
One	Page 134
One Day at a Time	Page 136
Our Dwelling Place in God	Page 138
Jesus	Page 140
Prayer to the Surgeon	Page 142
Redeemed	Page 144
Redemption	Page 146
Roots and Wings	Page 148
Sacrifice of Praise	Page 150

Salvation's Song	Page 152
Salvation	Page 154
Set Free	Page 156
Shepherd of the Kingdom	Page 158
Sometimes	Page 160
Lord Over All	Page 162
Taking the Risk	Page 164
Tapestry of Love	Page 166
That Is Why	Page 168
The Advent	Page 170
The Covenant	Page 172
The Abiding Place	Page 174
The All Sufficient One	Page 176
The Blessing	Page 178
The Blood Covenant	Page 180
The Bridegroom	Page 182
The Christmas Story	Page 184
The Class of '55	Page 186
The Coming Joy	Page 188
The Cry of the Soul	Page 190
The Divine Shepherd	Page 192
The Gift of a Friend	Page 194
The Gift of Choice	Page 195
The Greatest Is Love	Page 197
The Immaculate Heart	Page 199
The Kingdom Within	Page 201
The Light of Men	Page 203
The Lion and the Lamb	Page 204
The Marred Image	Page 206
The Master	Page 208
The Master Artist	Page 210
The Mind of God	Page 212
The Pearl of Great Price	Page 214
The Prize in the High Calling	Page 216
The Promise	Page 218
The Promise and the Gift	Page 220
The Road to the Unknown	Page 223
The Soul	Page 225

The Tree	Page 227
The Truth	Page 229
The Valley of Loss	Page 231
The Veil	Page 233
The Weaver	Page 235
The Wonder of Wonders	Page 237
Through the Eyes of Faith	Page 239
Time and Eternity	Page 242
Triumph in Jesus	Page 244
Trust	Page 246
Unveiled Mystery	Page 247
We Are Healed	Page 249
Yours Is the Kingdom	Page 251
You Are There	Page 253
Yearning	Page 255
Words of Life	Page 257